Celebrate
Diwali

Recipes, activities and crafts
to do with your kids

Celebrate
Diwali

Renu Bhardwaj

POP PRESS

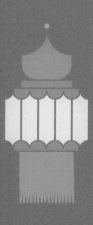

Gifts
117

EDIBLE GIFT IDEAS
129

Helpful extras
147

Crafts
81

Introduction

As autumn whispers through the chill air, I feel a spark of childlike excitement for Diwali. Soon, scents of cinnamon and cardamom will waft through our home as we prepare festive sweets and savouries. For five glimmering days, our family joins millions worldwide celebrating Diwali, the cherished festival of lights and the start of the Hindu new year.

Though I live worlds away from my mother's childhood in India, our home comes alive with the traditional rituals she encourages, lit up with the gentle glow of *diyas*, tiny flames welcoming the Hindu goddess Lakshmi's blessings, laughter filling our kitchen as we prepare *samosa chaat, chole bhatura* and Nanni's creamy *kheer* (you can find my recipes on pages 24, 32 and 59). We bridge generations through these recipes crafted with love.

In Hindu homes, families gather dressed in vibrant, jewel-toned saris and shining *sherwanis* – their finest traditional outfits. They perform puja rituals with plates laden with sweets, flowers, fruits and candles, offering prayers for health and prosperity. Temples and houses are lit up by thousands of *diyas* and clay lamps, a guiding path for Lakshmi as families welcome her blessings for the coming year. Vibrant rangoli patterns decorate entrances alongside marigold garlands, mango leaves and bright lights. Diwali is a time to think about our inner light and the value of leading a moral and purposeful life and I'm honoured to share a window into my family's traditions.

It is my hope that this book guides you in making your own meaningful Diwali memories. May these pages bring the calm reassurance of a trusted friend amid the bustle of obligations. Find joy reliving cherished customs while creating new rituals. Recreate decorative crafts you enjoyed as a child which in turn will spark precious memories within your children each year. Reignite nostalgia through aromas from the recipes, and watch precious bonds strengthen each year as you pass traditions to future generations.

Above all, I hope that this book helps deepen Diwali's gifts of family, wisdom, compassion and the light within that guides us through any dark days ahead. Happy Diwali and thank you for welcoming me into your home.

Why is Diwali celebrated?

Diwali is so much more than just a 'festival of lights'. Those of us who cherish its traditions know it illuminates far more than the night sky. Diwali honours the victory of light over darkness and good over evil. It is a celebration that reignites the light within us all – the light signifying family bonds, shared heritage and our common humanity. It reaffirms that light lies not just in the flickering flames of *diyas* but in the joy exchanged between loved ones.

What's more, Diwali is not solely an important religious festival for Hindus – it is also observed by Jains, Sikhs and Buddhists, and while each religion has its own story behind the festival, each celebration represents the same triumph of good over evil. Over five days, Hindus mark the return of deities Rama and Sita from exile (for the full story see page 14); Sikhs celebrate the freeing of the Guru Hargobind Singh from prison (see page 13); and Jains commemorate the attainment of *moksha* (eternal bliss) by Lord Mahavira.

WHY DO WE LIGHT DIYAS?

The *diya*, or oil lamp, symbolises the essence of Diwali. Each part of the *diya* represents a different Hindu goddess and her blessings. The oil that fuels the flame represents the prosperity and abundance granted by Lakshmi. The glowing light signifies the knowledge and wisdom bestowed by Saraswati. The protective heat radiating from the flame symbolises the strength and bravery of Durga.

The Hindu goddess Lakshmi holds special significance during Diwali celebrations. As the goddess of wealth, prosperity and good fortune, Lakshmi is worshipped and invited into homes. It is believed she visits each house on Diwali night to bestow blessings of wealth and success for the coming year. Hindus light *diyas* and candles throughout homes and temples during Diwali to welcome Lakshmi and show her reverence. It is thought that the abundant light guides her. The rows of flickering lights also represent the light of knowledge and truth dispelling the darkness of ignorance.

Lighting *diyas* during Diwali is also thought to purify a home. The sacred fire is believed to cleanse the space of negativity, making way for positivity and goodness, while the *diya*'s warmth combats humidity, safeguarding the home from harm. Through this simple act of lighting an oil lamp, Hindus create both a physically and spiritually purified space.

How is Diwali traditionally celebrated?

The Diwali festivities unfold over five auspicious days, each
with its own significance and traditions. The exact dates
change each year and are determined by the position of the
moon – but they usually fall between October and November.
    Dhanteras, the first day of Diwali, marks new beginnings.
People thoroughly clean their homes to welcome the festival.
Dhanteras honours the day when the god Dhanvantari
emerged from the Ocean of Milk holding a pot of *amrita*,
the nectar of immortality. Dhanteras also honours the legend
of a prince being saved from death by Lakshmi. Hindus begin
preparations for Lakshmi's prosperity by cleaning their homes
and making decorations. Traditionally, on this day people
buy gold, silver, utensils, appliances and vehicles. Gold is
considered a symbol of luck, prosperity and abundance.
    Choti Diwali (small Diwali), the second day, is when
preparations intensify. Families decorate their homes
with colourful rangoli floor designs and elaborate flower
garlands. *Diyas* are placed around the house and filled
with oil to prepare for the night ahead.
    Lakshmi Puja is the third and main Diwali festive day –
it is the one many Hindus refer to as Diwali when they

talk about the celebration. Lakshmi is worshipped and her blessings sought. *Diyas* illuminate every home, creating a glittering display. Friends and relatives visit each other, exchanging sweets and gifts. Prayers are offered to Lakshmi while children wear their best clothes and light sparklers; fireworks are often lit too.

Govardhan Puja is celebrated on the fourth day and honours Lord Krishna. Hindus celebrate this festival by reciting *bhajans* (songs) and offering different foods, sweets, flowers and *prasad* (see page 151).

Lastly, Bhai Dooj, on the fifth day, celebrates the unbreakable bond between siblings. On this special occasion brothers and sisters come together to strengthen their relationship. Sisters apply *tilak* (often referred to as *tika* colloquially), a mark made from a coloured powder or paste, to their brothers' foreheads, and pray for their brothers' wellbeing, longevity and prosperity. In return, brothers give gifts to their sisters and spend quality time with them, often celebrating with a shared meal. I have fond memories of gathering with my brother and cousins to commemorate the day. Now, it brings me great joy to see my own children appreciate and participate in this meaningful tradition.

WHAT IS *BANDI CHHOR DIVAS*?

Bandi Chhor Divas is celebrated by Sikhs on the same day as Diwali. The festival commemorates the day the sixth Sikh Guru, Guru Hargobind, was released from imprisonment in Gwalior fort in 1619 along with 52 Hindu kings. Guru Hargobind agreed to be released only if the 52 kings he was in prison with could come with him. The Mughal Emperor Jahangir said he could bring along with him as many prisoners as could hold on to his cloak so Guru Hargobind had a cloak made with 52 tassels attached to it.

The Guru had found a way to get 52 of these innocent leaders released from the prison without a battle.

Bandi Chhor Divas and Diwali are separate festivals, though in most popular calendars they are sometimes observed on the same day. In real terms, the day of Guru Hargobind's release was actually a few days before Diwali in 1619. The festival is celebrated with great enthusiasm by Sikhs worldwide. The story is a reminder of the importance of freedom and human rights, and the triumph of good over evil. The celebrations include lighting up homes and gurdwaras with candles and *diyas*, singing hymns and offering prayers.

Diwali made simple: explaining the story of Diwali to children

For those with children, this section will help you explain the story and traditions of Diwali to them in a fun, short and memorable narrative they will adore: long ago in ancient India, there was a brave and noble prince named Rama. He lived happily in the kingdom of Ayodhya with his beautiful wife Sita and his loyal brother Lakshmana. But one day, the selfish king told Rama he had to leave the kingdom and live in the forest for 14 years. Rama accepted this unfair punishment and left for the forest with Sita and Lakshmana.

While in the forest, an evil demon named Ravana found Sita alone and decided to kidnap her. He took her away to his faraway island. Poor Rama was so sad that Sita was gone, but he didn't lose hope. He gathered an army of magical monkeys to help him find Sita. After a big battle between Rama and Ravana, Rama shot a powerful arrow that defeated the demon. Finally, Sita was free.

Villagers were so happy that Rama and Sita were back together, so to guide their way home, they lit small clay lamps called *diyas*. This is how the festival of Diwali began. On Diwali, the *diyas* remind us of Rama's bravery and of the victory of good over evil. They also represent the light of hope, goodness and wisdom inside us all.

This is why Diwali is called the festival of lights. The *diyas* spread light to conquer darkness, just like Rama did. Diwali teaches us never to give up hope.

How to host a Diwali dinner

A big part of Diwali's celebrations are centred around food. If you're hosting a Diwali celebration, here are some suggestions to make it a memorable one.

MENU

Choosing the right menu for your celebration can be a delicate task. The key is to strike a harmonious balance between traditional dishes and more contemporary, crowd-pleasing options. When planning your menu, consider choosing some dishes that can be prepped the night before – several of the recipes that follow can be prepared ahead. Create some exciting mocktails to complement the flavours of your Diwali feast. If you have time, handwritten menus are a lovely personal touch.

WELCOME MOCKTAILS

Welcome your guests with a refreshing drink that's ready when they arrive, this really sets the tone for the Diwali celebration. It's a great fuss-free way to greet your guests, leaving you more time to continue your evening preparations. Check out the mocktail suggestions on pages 70, 74 and 75.

DECORATIONS

Add colour to your table with tablecloths and napkins, charger plates and placemats. Keep festivities bright with strings of fairy lights, colourful lanterns and flickering *diyas* that instantly create a warming ambience. For an extra-special welcome, create a spectacular entrance piece that features an immense rangoli design (see pages 98 and 110) or position a statue of Ganesh illuminated with hand-decorated tealights (see page 104).

EASY CENTREPIECES

Keep this simple by using existing floral arrangements you may have around the house or some tealights in holders. You can also use large hurricane lamps. For lots of decorative inspiration have a glance through the Crafts chapter (see page 81).

Diwali games and activities

Diwali is all about celebration, so be sure to plan some fun activities, games and entertainment to keep the party going. Have a list of games ready that are suitable for all ages. Card games, such as *Bhabhi*, are a classic choice, or sing your hearts out by playing *Antakshari*. Many Diwali celebrations often involve a bit of light-hearted gambling as well, so be sure to have some extra cash on hand. Just keep it friendly and remember it's all in good spirit!

For an added touch of creativity, you can host a Diwali-themed crafting session where guests can showcase their artistic talents by painting their own tealight candles (see page 104). At the end, they'll get to take home their handmade creations.

THOUGHTFUL FAVOURS

If you really want to make your guests feel special this Diwali, there's nothing better than a personal touch. You could make edible gifts (you'll find my recipes on pages 129–142), or get creative with handcrafted items, like the beautiful lanterns (see page 103) or hand-painted tealights (see page 104), which you can place in organza bags or gift boxes, along with handwritten thank you notes. These small gestures will make everyone feel truly appreciated for celebrating this special occasion with you.

MUSIC AND DANCE

It's worth spending time putting together a playlist before your guests arrive. You can end the night playing your favourite Indian tracks, including Bollywood classics, which will encourage everyone to get up and dance!

ENTERTAINMENT

Have a firework display to finish off the night's festivities and let the younger kids have some sparkler fun; I find sticking the sparklers into carrots makes them easier for the children to handle.

Introduction

Recipes

Recipes

This chapter is an invitation into my kitchen. You will discover treasured family recipes handed down over the years. There are also fresh takes that fuse flavours in new ways while keeping tradition alive, such as the vibrant *samosa chaat* and Masala chips (see pages 24 and 36).

Food at Diwali is so much more than nourishment; it represents cherished traditions and a profound act of love poured into each bowl. The comforting aromas and familiar flavours of Diwali treats have the power to transport us, sparking feelings of warmth and nostalgia. With one bite, memories of the heady scents of spices and helping to roll out soft naan and fluffy bhatura come flooding back. As rich sweets like *ladoo* (see page 134)

and creamy *kheer* (see page 59) melt in our mouths, we are children again, bonding with loved ones over the buzzing energy of activity in the kitchen. By passing down these recipes from one generation to the next, we honour the legacies of our families and cultures.

Follow these recipes as they are or or make them using ingredients that are readily available or mean something special to you. Most importantly, let the act of cooking nourish your own Diwali traditions and bonds.

Cook the curries and the dal at least a day earlier to allow their flavours to develop. Let the recipes help you create your perfect Diwali feast.

Starters

Samosa chaat

Samosa chaat is a play on the traditional street food *papri chaat*, and I love to make it on most gatherings. It is a vegetarian dish that is made by taking samosas and smashing them, then serving them over a bed of *chole* (spiced chickpeas). The dish is then topped with layers of flavoured yoghurt, mint and coriander chutney, pomegranates, sev and coriander. This is one of my favourite ways to eat samosas; it makes a great starter – a family-friendly platter that you can prepare ahead of time.

SERVES 4

200–300ml Greek
    yoghurt, whisked
1 tsp ground coriander
1 tsp chaat masala
4 vegetable samosas, slightly
    smashed down and cut
    into in 4 big chunks
3 tbsp mint and coriander
    chutney (see page 50)
3 spring onions, finely chopped
handful of fine sev or Bombay
    mix (optional but highly
    recommended)
sea salt and black pepper

FOR THE SPICED CHICKPEAS

2 tbsp rapeseed oil
1 tsp cumin seeds
2 garlic cloves, crushed
    or finely chopped
2.5cm piece of ginger,
    peeled and grated
1 x 400g can of chickpeas,
    drained
¾ tsp ground turmeric
½ tsp chilli powder
1½ tsp ground cumin
1 x black teabag
    (I use an everyday tea,
    such as Tetley or PG Tips)
handful of coriander, chopped

FOR THE QUICK PICKLED ONIONS

1 small red onion, finely sliced
juice of 1 lemon
3 tbsp white vinegar
½ tsp salt
½ tsp sugar

1. Start by making the quick pickled onions. Place the onion in a heatproof bowl, cover with just boiled water and leave for 10 minutes. Drain, then add the lemon juice, vinegar, salt and sugar and set aside. The onions will turn a wonderful pink colour.

2. Next, make the spiced chickpeas. Heat the oil in a saucepan over a medium heat. Add the cumin seeds and allow to sizzle, then add the garlic and ginger. Cook for 2 minutes, until golden brown, then add the spices and cook for a further minute.

3. Add the chickpeas and 70ml of hot water. Add the teabag, cover and simmer over a low heat for about 15 minutes, or until the flavours have infused. Remove the teabag, gently mash some of the chickpeas in the pan to thicken the sauce. Finish by checking the seasoning and topping with the chopped coriander.

4. Mix the yoghurt with the ground coriander and chaat masala and season with salt and pepper to taste.

5. Spoon the spiced chickpeas on to a serving platter and layer the samosas over the top. Drizzle over the seasoned yoghurt, mint and coriander chutney, then top with the pickled onions. Sprinkle over the chopped spring onions and sev or Bombay mix to give you that crunch.

Spicy potato balls

This is an effortless cross between an *aloo tiki* and a healthier version of *batata vada* (spiced potato ball fritters). The balls have an extremely soft, spicy filling and a crispy covering. They can be prepared in advance and baked in the oven and are best served with my scrumptious mint and coriander chutney (see page 50). I like to turn any leftovers into mini spicy sandwiches for lunch – they are delicious with some chutney, salad and even more indulgent with a little cheese.

MAKES ABOUT 18-20 BALLS

500g small baby potatoes, peeled
1 red chilli, finely chopped (adjust the amount according to your taste)
3 spring onions, finely chopped
handful of coriander, finely chopped
juice of ½ lemon
3 tbsp olive oil
1 tsp chilli powder
1 tsp ground turmeric
1 tsp garam masala
1 tsp ground cumin
1 tsp smoked paprika
1 tbsp sea salt
2 tbsp cornflour
2 tbsp rice flour
vegetable oil, for baking
Mint and coriander chutney (see page 50), to serve

1. Place the potatoes in a pan of salted cold water and bring to a gentle boil. Boil until soft – about 15–18 minutes, depending on your potatoes. They should be soft all the way through; you can test this by piercing them with a skewer. Once cooked, drain and allow to cool.

2. Transfer the potatoes to a large bowl and mash them until very smooth. I use a potato ricer for a smoother finish.

3. Preheat your oven to 180°C fan. Line a baking tray with baking paper.

4. Add all the remaining ingredients except the oil to the bowl of potato and mix well; they should bind together and become a soft dough.

5. Oil your hands lightly to avoid the dough sticking to them, then take 1 tablespoon of the potato mixture and roll it in your hands to form a ball, then repeat until you have used up all the mixture. Try to keep the balls the same size for consistency of cooking.

6. Place on the baking tray and drizzle with a little oil.

7. Bake in the oven for 15–20 minutes or until golden brown. Shake the tray halfway through the cooking time for even colouring.

8. The balls also freeze well for up to 3 months once cooked, or you can freeze the uncooked balls for up to 6 months. Defrost by allowing them to soften at room temperature for 1–2 hours, then cook as above. Reheat the cooked balls in an oven set to 180°C fan for 10–15 minutes.

Chilli paneer

Paneer is unquestionably one of the most popular foods in an Indian household. Chilli paneer is an Indo-Chinese favourite of crispy cheese tossed in spicy, salty, sweet and sour sauces. I believe every household serves their own version of this as it's so easy to make and full of flavour – a guaranteed crowd-pleaser. Chilli paneer can be served as a starter alone or it works well as a main course served with some basmati rice or naan.

SERVES 4

2 x blocks of paneer, roughly
  200–230g each, cut into
  2cm cubes
1 tbsp chaat masala
1 tbsp cornflour
½ tsp sea salt
1 tbsp vegetable oil

FOR THE CHILLI STIR FRY

1 tbsp vegetable oil
3 spring onions, finely
  sliced, whites and
  greens separated
3–4 garlic cloves, finely
  chopped or crushed
2.5cm piece of ginger,
  peeled and finely chopped
  or crushed
1 green chilli, slit lengthways
2 medium peppers
  (1 red and 1 green), cut into
  chunky squares
1 red onion, cut into quarters,
  leaves separated

FOR THE SAUCE

1 tsp dark soy sauce
2 tbsp light soy sauce
2 tbsp tomato ketchup
1 tbsp rice vinegar
  or lemon juice
1 tbsp Szechuan sauce
  or chilli sauce of choice
1 tsp clear honey
1 tsp cornflour mixed with
  3 tbsp water

1. For a paneer with a soft texture, start by soaking it in boiling water and letting it sit for at least 20 minutes in a container covered with a lid to ensure the paneer stays hot. Drain and pat dry.

2. Transfer the paneer to a bowl and mix with the chaat masala, cornflour, salt and oil until evenly coated.

3. Heat a large frying pan or wok over a medium heat and fry the paneer in batches so that you don't crowd the pan and it cooks evenly. Fry until golden on all sides, then remove and wipe out the pan.

4. For the chilli stir fry, reheat the pan over a medium–high heat, add the oil then your spring onion whites, garlic, ginger and chilli and sauté for roughly 1 minute, stirring constantly to prevent any sticking.

5. Add the peppers, red onion and the paneer and sauté for a further minute. Garnish with the spring onion greens and serve immediately.

Mains

Chole bhatura

Spicy chickpeas with fried bread

The irresistible combination of spiced chickpeas and puffy, deep-fried bread makes *chole bhatura* a cherished and very popular Punjabi dish, especially at Diwali. Chickpeas are simmered and infused with aromatics and spices, and the dough needs to rest before being fried to create the pillowy *bhatura*, so I reserve this for special occasions like Diwali. *Chole bhatura* is also sure to wow guests with its layers of flavours and textures, bringing a celebratory mood and an atmosphere of joy, gratitude and togetherness – and that crisp, hot-from-the-pan bread always tempts me into a gratifying second helping. I'm delighted to share my take on this special dish so that you can savour its spirit at your own gatherings. You can make the *chole* two days before you wish to serve it and the *bhatura* dough a day earlier, but the *bhatura* are best fried just before serving so that you can enjoy them hot.

SERVES 3-4

FOR THE CHOLE

2 x 400g cans of chickpeas,
    drained
2 garlic cloves, sliced
1 black teabag or 2 tbsp loose
    tea tied in a muslin cloth
    (I use an everyday tea such
    as Tetley, PG Tips or an
    English Breakfast teabag)
1 cinnamon stick
2 or 3 whole cloves
1 star anise
2 black cardamom pods
1 bay leaf
2 tbsp rapeseed oil or other
    cooking oil
1 tsp cumin seeds
2.5cm piece of ginger, peeled
    and cut into very fine
    matchsticks, plus a little
    extra to serve
1 white onion, finely chopped
1 tsp amchur
    (dried mango powder)
1 tsp anardana
    (pomegranate powder)
½ tsp ground turmeric
3 tbsp tomato purée
1 tbsp ground coriander
1 tbsp chana masala
    (optional but highly
    recommended if you
    have some)
1-2 green chillies, sliced
    (adjust the amount
    according to your taste),
    plus an optional extra one
    to garnish
sea salt
small handful of coriander,
    finely chopped, to serve

FOR THE BHATURA

150g self-raising flour, sifted
300g semolina
2-3 tbsp vegetable oil,
    plus more for deep frying
1½ tsp baking powder
1 tsp sea salt
1 tsp granulated sugar
125g plain yoghurt
100ml warm water, plus
    a little extra as needed

1. Start by making the *chole*. Add the drained chickpeas, garlic, tea bag, cinnamon, cloves, star anise, cardamom and bay leaf to a medium saucepan and pour in enough cold water to cover generously. Bring to a simmer and cook, uncovered, for 10 minutes. Remove from the heat and set aside to allow the flavours to infuse.

2. Heat the oil in another pan over a medium heat. Once hot, add the cumin seeds. When the seeds start to crackle, add the ginger and fry for a minute.

3. Add the onion and sauté until golden brown. Now add the amchur, anardana and turmeric and cook for 2 more minutes.

4. Next, add the tomato purée and mix everything well. Cook for 5 minutes or until the raw smell of tomatoes is gone, stirring occasionally to prevent the mixture from sticking to the pan.

5. Now add the ground coriander, chana masala and chillies. Mix everything well again and cook for 5-6 minutes until you can see the sauce coming together.

6. Remove the teabag, whole spices and bay leaf from the cooked chickpeas, pour the spicy sauce into their pan and mix well until combined. At this point, check for consistency – the sauce should not be dry, so add 3-4 tablespoons of water if it needs a little more liquid. Cook over a low heat for 7-8 minutes, then turn off the heat and set it aside while you make the bhatura.

7. To make the *bhatura*, sift the flour into a large mixing bowl, add the semolina and mix well to combine. You can either do this by hand or in your stand mixer fitted with a dough hook.

8. Add the oil, baking powder, salt and sugar and mix well before adding the yoghurt and mixing again. Slowly add the warm water, a little at a time, and knead into a firm wet dough. It should come together so that it is not too sticky and forms a ball.

9. Once the dough is ready, apply a little oil to it, then cover the bowl with a tea towel and set it aside for 2–3 hours in a warm place for the dough to rise.

10. After resting, punch down the dough and transfer it to a work surface. Put some vegetable oil into a small bowl next to you. Cover your fingers in oil and spread this over the surface of the dough, then divide the dough into 6–8 equal portions.

11. Lightly oil a rolling pin, then roll each piece of dough out into an oval shape no more than 1cm thick. Do the same with each of the dough balls.

12. Pour vegetable oil into a large deep wok, saucepan or karahi until it is three quarters full. Heat the oil on a high heat until it reaches 180°C. If you don't have a thermometer you can test this by dropping a small piece of dough into the oil; it should brown and rise to the top in a few seconds.

13. Once the oil is hot, gently slide a *bhatura* into the oil using a slotted spoon. Press the centre lightly with the spoon; this will help the *bhatura* to puff up. Once it forms a bubble, flip it over on to the other side and cook, continuing to turn it, until pale golden brown. Remove the fried *bhatura* using the slotted spoon and transfer it to kitchen paper to drain. Once you have made the first, the rest will cook faster so turn the heat down to medium and repeat.

14. When all the *bhatura* have been fried, reheat the *chole* gently and scatter over the chopped coriander and the extra ginger matchsticks or a green chilli for garnish.

Masala chips

This is a flavour-packed dish – crispy chips coated in a spicy tomato sauce and topped with fresh chillies and herbs. While they may not grace my table on a regular basis, the aromatic bites of these spicy chips hold a special place in my heart, evoking cherished memories of family gatherings and the comfort of Diwali celebrations.

SERVES 4

3 large potatoes, peeled and sliced into chips (I cut mine into 7 x 1cm chips but you can cut yours as thick as you like them)
cornflour, for dusting
vegetable oil, for deep-frying
sliced spring onion, to garnish

FOR THE BATTER

1 tbsp cornflour
3 tbsp plain flour
½ tsp sea salt
150ml water

FOR THE SPICY SAUCE

2 tbsp rapeseed or vegetable oil
1 tsp sesame seeds, plus extra to garnish
3 garlic cloves, finely chopped or crushed
½ medium onion, finely sliced
½ green pepper, finely sliced
3 tsp tomato ketchup
2 tsp sriracha sauce
3 tsp soy sauce
1 tsp caster sugar
1 tsp sea salt
2 tsp clear honey
2 tsp cornflour mixed with 2 tsp water

1. Add the potatoes to a large saucepan of cold salted water, bring to the boil and simmer for 7 minutes. You are only partially cooking them so they will not be cooked through. Drain and leave to dry and cool. Once cooled dust with a little cornflour.

2. Mix the batter ingredients well in a bowl, ensuring there are no lumps. You should have a thick smooth consistency.

3. In a large bowl, coat the chips in the batter.

4. Pour the vegetable oil into a large deep wok, saucepan or karahi until it is three quarters full. Heat the oil on a high heat until it reaches 180°C. If you don't have a thermometer you can test the heat by dropping some of the batter into the oil – if it is ready it will rise with a sizzle. Carefully add half the chips to the oil and fry for 3–4 minutes turning them as they cook. The chips will stick together but you can break them up later. Once brown and cooked through, drain with a slotted spoon on kitchen paper. Cook the second batch, then set aside while you make the sauce.

5. The sauce cooks quickly so have everything ready to avoid it burning. Place a wok over a high heat, add the oil and toast the sesame seeds. After 30 seconds add the garlic and mix well.

6. Add the onion and pepper and cook for 1 minute, then add the tomato ketchup, sriracha, soy sauce, sugar and salt and mix.

7. Stir in the cornflour paste to thicken, then add the honey and mix again before adding the chips. Turn them to ensure they are coated in the sauce.

8. Garnish with a sprinkling of sesame seeds and spring onion and enjoy.

Dal makhani

Slow-cooked black lentils

Punjabi *dal makhani* is a delicious, rich and creamy dish made with black lentils, spices, butter and cream. It holds an esteemed place at the table, reserved for celebratory occasions. Taking hours of meticulous preparation, each pot simmers with labour and love and the dal's indulgent essence signifies moments of meaning – milestones marked and achievements honoured. At gatherings like Diwali, the aroma of *dal makhani* beckons all to celebrate, it is an offering conveying the care and intention you extend to your guests through food. Serve this with rice and naan.

SERVES 6

160g whole urad dal
    (black lentils)
45g dried kidney beans
1 slice ginger, peeled, plus
    5cm piece of ginger,
    peeled and grated
2 green chillies, 1 left whole,
    1 finely chopped
handful of coriander,
    finely chopped
80ml cream (whichever
    type you prefer), to serve
sea salt

FOR THE TARKA MASALA

3 tbsp butter (to make
    it less rich you can use
    vegetable oil)
½ tsp cumin seeds
2–3 whole cloves
2–3 green cardamoms
1 black cardamom
2.5cm piece of cinnamon stick
1 Indian bay leaf
1 onion, finely chopped
3 garlic cloves, crushed
    or finely chopped (optional)
½ tsp red kashmiri chilli
    or smoked paprika
¼ tsp crushed kasuri methi
    (dry fenugreek leaves)
2–3 pinches of grated
    nutmeg or ground nutmeg
130ml passata

1. Wash the lentils and kidney beans several times until the water runs clear. Put in a large bowl and cover with plenty of warm water, at least double the quantity of lentils. Allow to soak overnight.

2. Put the lentils and kidney beans into a large saucepan with 1.5 litres of water. Add the slice of ginger, 1 whole chilli and bring to a boil. To make a really creamy, rich dal, it is best to simmer this very slowly, on a low heat for 3–4 hours, until the dal is soft, but if you've soaked the beans overnight, they will be cooked through in 1 hour – they will just have more of a bite. You can also cook this in a slow cooker for 7–8 hours on the high setting. The secret to this dal is this process of slow cooking, so the longer you can cook this on low heat the more luxurious and creamier the dal will be. Remove the ginger and chilli. Using a large open whisk or fork, stir the dal with a whisk or fork to break up any large chunks – this also mashes some of the dal and releases a natural creaminess from the lentils, which helps create a richer base.

3. To make the tarka masala, heat the butter in a separate pan over a medium-high heat and add the cumin seeds, cloves, green cardamoms, black cardamom, cinnamon and bay leaf. Fry the spices until they sizzle and smell aromatic. Add the onion and cook for 5 minutes over a medium heat until it turns pale golden.

4. Add the ginger and garlic, if using, and cook until just brown before adding the chopped chilli and the remaining spices. Add the passata and cook for 5 minutes, until it turns a dark red colour and you see a film of oil appear on the top of the liquid. Stir the tarka masala into the cooked dal.

5. Add 250ml of water to the dal and allow it to simmer for 25 minutes on a low heat. This allows the dal to loosen up and brings together the masala and the lentils and kidney beans.

6. To serve, scatter over the coriander, and add a swirl of cream.

Achari aloo

Pickled spiced potatoes

In any Indian home, you can always find a potato dish gracing the table, a *sabji* (vegetable dish) that infuses a meal with comfort. *Achari aloo* is a tasty Punjabi dish made using pickling spices that raise the humble potato to new heights. These tangy potatoes have been a staple at my family's feasts for as long as I can remember and they are a crowd-pleaser. Serve alongside a dal with raita and naan (see pages 38, 52 and 55).

SERVES 4–5

900g small baby potatoes, peeled
1 tsp rapeseed oil
½ lemon
handful of coriander, chopped

FOR THE WHOLE SPICES

1 tsp cumin seeds
1 tsp coriander seeds
1 tsp black mustard seeds
½ tsp fennel seeds
½ tsp carom (ajwain) seeds
¼ tsp fenugreek seeds
2 dried red chillies

FOR THE SAUCE

2 tbsp rapeseed oil
1 tsp cumin seeds
½ tsp mustard seeds
1 tsp garlic, finely chopped or crushed
1 tsp grated ginger
¾ tsp ground turmeric
1 tsp red chilli powder
1 tsp amchur powder or chaat masala
1 tsp sea salt

1. Place the potatoes in a saucepan of salted cold water and bring to a gentle boil, then simmer gently until soft – about 10 minutes, depending on your potatoes. They should be soft all the way through; you can test this by piercing the potatoes with a skewer. Once cooked, drain and allow to cool.

2. Using a fork, make small indents in the potatoes, which will allow the sauce to penetrate the flesh and give the potatoes maximum flavour.

3. In a large wok or frying pan, dry-roast the whole spices. Once you can smell the aromas – after 2–3 minutes – remove the pan from the heat and blitz into a powder using a spice grinder or by hand with a pestle and mortar.

4. Add the 1 teaspoon of oil to the same pan and fry the baby potatoes over a medium heat for 4–5 minutes, until they turn golden brown, then remove from the pan.

5. Make the sauce by adding the oil, cumin seeds, mustard seeds, garlic and ginger to the same pan. Cook over a medium heat until just brown – about 1–2 minutes. Add the remaining spices and mix, then return the potatoes to the pan.

6. Add the blended spice powder and coat the potatoes well, then cook for a further 2 minutes. Remove the pan from the heat and serve the potatoes with a squeeze of lemon and sprinkled with coriander.

Paneer biryani

Biryani needs no introduction, it's a classic, comforting Indian one-pot dish. Here paneer is layered with vegetables and cooked to perfection in fragrant basmati rice that's flavoured with fresh coriander, mint and whole spices. This dish does take quite a while to prepare as there are several processes but the meticulous task of layering rice, paneer and spices reflects the care with which you bring the pot to life. Serving it is a smile of appreciation for the guests at your table. Serve the biryani with raita and *kachumber* salad (see pages 52 and 48) and *achari aloo* (see page 41), if wished.

SERVES 5-6

2 pinches of saffron threads
4 tbsp whole or semi-
    skimmed milk
1–2 tsp salt
450g long-grain basmati rice
½ tsp garam masala

FOR THE BIRYANI SAUCE

20 cashew nuts
6 tbsp rapeseed oil
2 x blocks of paneer,
    roughly 200–230g each
2 white onions, thinly sliced
1 large green pepper,
    thinly sliced
1 tsp grated ginger
1 tsp garlic paste
    or 1 garlic clove, crushed
1 chilli, finely chopped
1 tsp salt
1½ tsp biryani powder
1 tsp ground coriander
½ tsp ground turmeric
1 tsp ground cumin
1 tsp Kashmiri powder
    or smoked paprika
2 tomatoes, roughly chopped
250g plain yoghurt
30g mint leaves,
    finely chopped
30g coriander, finely chopped

FOR THE WHOLE SPICES

2 bay leaves
2 star anise
6 green cardamoms
1 cinnamon stick, broken in half

1. The key to this dish is prepping everything ahead. Have your ingredients prepared, ready to be added to the dish.

2. Put the saffron and milk into a small bowl and keep to the side.

3. Rinse the rice thoroughly. My mum always advised me to rinse it at least 5 times to remove the starch by placing it in a large bowl, adding cold water and swirling the water in a circular motion with my hand to release the starch, then draining the water and repeating another 4 times. After rinsing, place it in a bowl of fresh water and soak for 30 minutes.

4. Start by making the biryani sauce. Heat a large deep frying pan and dry-fry the cashew nuts over a medium heat. Once brown remove from the pan. Add 2 tablespoons of the oil to the pan and heat gently over a medium heat, then add the paneer. Gently fry on both sides until golden brown. Remove from the heat and keep to the side. Once cooled, cut into 1cm cubes.

5. Measure out 875ml of water, pour it into a separate pan and add the salt, then add the rice and bring to the boil. Cook for 15 minutes or until al dente – the rice has been soaking so it won't need that long to cook. Drain the rice and keep to the side.

6. Add the remaining oil to the pan and cook the onions over a medium heat until brown, stirring to avoid them burning. Remove 2 tablespoons of the onions and set them aside for the garnish, then add the ginger, garlic and chilli to the pan. Add the whole spices and cook for another 2–3 minutes.

7. Add the salt, biryani powder, ground coriander, turmeric, cumin and Kashmiri powder, then add the tomatoes and cook for 4–5 minutes until the colour changes and the sauce comes together so it's a thick tomato paste.

8. Turn the heat to low, add the yoghurt and mix well. Cook on a low heat for 3–4 minutes, until you can see a film of oil on top.

9. Taste the sauce to check the seasoning, adding more salt if necessary. At this point add 150ml of water to the pan to ensure the sauce isn't too thick, as this sauce stays at the bottom of the pan closest to the heat. Add the paneer and mix well to coat it in the sauce, then remove 2 tablespoons of the coated paneer. Stir in a third of the mint and coriander, keeping some for garnishing.

10. Spoon the hot cooked rice over the yoghurt biryani pressing down a little with the back of a spoon.

11. Pour the saffron milk over the rice, then sprinkle over the toasted cashews, reserved paneer, then sprinkle over the garam masala.

12. Cover the pan securely using foil, then place a tea towel on a work surface and the lid in the middle of the tea towel, then bring the four corners of the tea towel up around the lid to wrap it like a present. Cover the foil with this; it acts as a double covering for the pan, which creates a steam effect during the cooking.

13. Cook the biryani on a medium heat for 2 minutes, then place the pan on a large flat pan or frying pan over a low heat. This is called dum heat cooking and cooks the rice slowly to prevent it burning and being over-cooked. Remove from the heat and allow the rice to sit in the steam for 10 minutes. This allows all the flavours to develop and deepen.

14. Carefully remove the covering – it will be hot. Garnish with the reserved mint and coriander, then using a large serving spoon, dig deep and serve all the layers so that every bite is a mouthful of flavour.

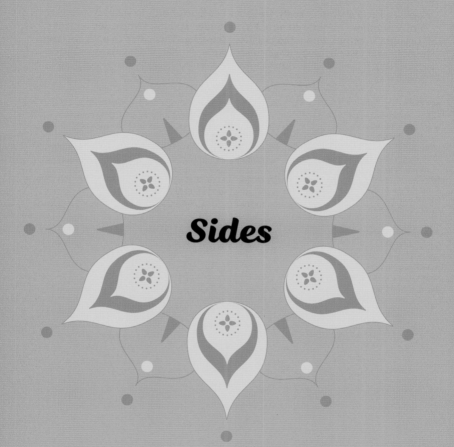

Sides

Kachumber salad

Simple Indian chopped salad

Kachumber is a simple, zesty, fresh and colourful Indian salad containing a mix of onion, tomato, cucumber, coriander and mint and a few spices, all brought together with a tangy citrus dressing. This salad is both relaxing to chop and visually appealing on any table. It pairs well with any starter, curry or main course.

SERVES 4

1 onion, finely chopped
5–6 mini or Persian
    cucumbers, or 1 large
    cucumber, finely chopped
150g tomatoes (a mix of small
    and large), finely chopped
handful of coriander,
    finely chopped
handful of mint,
    finely chopped

FOR THE DRESSING

juice of ½ lemon
juice of 1 lime
½ tsp ground cumin
½ tsp kala namak
sea salt and pepper

1. Soak the chopped onion in hot water in a bowl for 5 minutes to remove any sharpness, then drain well and squeeze out any excess liquid.

2. Place it in a serving bowl along with all the remaining salad ingredients.

3. To make the dressing, put all the ingredients into a jug or glass jar. Season with salt and pepper to taste and mix well before pouring over the salad.

Mint and coriander chutney

I don't recall a time growing up when we didn't have a jar of this in our fridge. It's become a go-to chutney that works with all cuisines. For an instant pick-me-up snack my mum and I would enjoy this on some hot buttery toast with a cup of tea, and I still love to enjoy my chutney this way. If you are lucky enough to grow mint in your garden during the summer, be sure to make a large batch of this chutney and freeze it. Make it ahead of time for any dinner occasion.

MAKES ABOUT 220ML

80g mint
50g coriander
¼ white onion
3 spring onions, trimmed
½ red chilli
juice of 1 lemon
1 tsp sea salt
1 tsp chilli powder
1 tsp garam masala
1 tsp chaat masala
1 tsp ground cumin
1 tsp mint sauce, or use
    1 tsp sugar
1 ice cube or 2–3 tbsp
    cold water
1 tbsp plain yoghurt (optional)

1. Put all the ingredients except the yoghurt into a blender and blend until smooth. If it is too thick and won't blend, add 2–3 tablespoons of water. You should be looking for a smooth, runny mixture (not like a pesto). Check the seasoning, adding salt if necessary, then transfer to an airtight glass container until ready to use.

2. When serving, transfer the amount you want to a serving dish and stir through the yoghurt then eat this within 2–3 days. Alternatively, you can keep the chutney without the yoghurt for up to 2 weeks in the airtight container in the fridge. Enjoy with anything!

Cucumber and cumin raita

Raita is a traditional Indian side dish that is always served alongside other curries to balance the heat. There are numerous flavour variations, ranging from yoghurt simply seasoned with salt and pepper, to versions including cucumber and spices. This recipe is the latter, and it's a personal favourite. When I was growing up, raita was a must-have on our dinner table, balancing the dals and *sabjis* (vegetables to accompany the lentils) that my mother would prepare every day. I was always in charge of making raita, and I believe I have mastered all of the varieties. Sometimes I like to finish this one with some pomegranate seeds, which look like jewels against the greenery.

SERVES 4

1½ tsp cumin seeds
200g plain or Greek yoghurt
½ cucumber, with skin,
   coarsely grated
1½ tsp sea salt
1 tsp black pepper
1½ tsp chaat masala
small handful of coriander,
   finely chopped

1. In a small frying pan, dry-roast the cumin seeds for 2–3 minutes until they begin to pop and you can smell the aroma. Grind them in a blender or simply wrap them in paper and roll a rolling pin over them.

2. Put the yoghurt, cucumber, salt, pepper and chaat masala into a serving bowl. Add the ground cumin seeds and mix well.

3. If the yoghurt is too thick add 2 tablespoons of water to loosen it. Finish with a sprinkle of coriander and keep the raita in the fridge until serving.

Naan and garlic naan

Soft, fluffy and delicious, homemade naan can be ready in under 10 minutes. I enjoy cooking these all the time and believe that this simple recipe can be used for any occasion.

MAKES 8 NAAN

175g self-raising flour, sifted, plus extra for dusting
½ tsp sea salt
250g Greek yoghurt
125ml water
1 tbsp butter or ghee, for brushing

FOR GARLIC NAAN

2 tbsp butter or ghee, melted, or olive oil
2-3 garlic cloves, grated or crushed
2 tbsp chopped coriander

1. In a large mixing bowl, combine the flour, salt and Greek yoghurt. Mix well, until combined. Slowly begin to add the water and knead the dough – you might not need all of the water so add it gradually. Knead the dough using stretch and pull movements for about 5 minutes until it comes together to form a lovely soft, smooth ball.

2. Lightly flour a clean kitchen work surface. Flatten the dough into a circular shape and divide it into 8 even portions. Flatten each portion into an oval or circle shape.

3. Heat a large non-stick frying pan or griddle on a medium heat. When hot, add a flattened piece of dough and cook for 3 minutes – you will know when to flip it as tiny little air bubbles will form around the edges of the dough. Flip it over and you will see big air bubbles begin to rise. Cook for a further 2 minutes as more bubbles rise on this side. To check the naan is cooked through, when you flip it over again, the naan should be light brown with charred pockets. Repeat until every naan is cooked, then wrap them in a tea towel to keep them warm.

4. Once cooked, melt the butter in a small pan and lightly brush the tops of each naan.

5. To make garlic naan, combine the melted butter, ghee or the oil with the garlic, coriander and a pinch of salt and brush over the cooked naan.

Desserts

Nanni's kheer
Grandma's rice pudding

Indian *kheer* is an instant bowl of love that fills you with gratitude and comfort. Of all desserts, nothing compares to the soul-warming joy of my mother's *kheer*, passed down through generations, from my nanni ji (my mum's mum). Love simmers in each pot of this quintessential Indian pudding. *Kheer* is traditionally prepared as *prasad* to bless Diwali celebrations through its sweet simplicity. *Kheer*'s basic elements lend themselves to being added to with endless flavour combinations, such as mango, pistachios or saffron. The options for infusing the pudding with your own twist are endless.

SERVES 4-5

200g short-grain pudding rice or basmati rice
1.5 litres whole milk
2-3 cardamoms (according to your taste), seeds removed from the pods and ground in a pestle and mortar
225g granulated sugar
sliced almonds and pistachios, to decorate

1. If you are using basmati rice, you will need to begin by washing the rice in a bowl to break it down. Fill the bowl with cold water and swirl the rice around to remove the starch, drain and repeat 4 more times, then soak the rinsed rice in water for 30 minutes and drain. If you are using pudding rice, it can be used without soaking.

2. Bring the milk to a boil in a large saucepan, then add the drained rice and cardamom. Cook for 30 minutes over a high heat, stirring continuously to prevent it from sticking to the bottom of the pan or boiling over.

3. Reduce the heat to medium, stir in the sugar and cook for another 30–45 minutes, stirring continuously. You'll know it's done when the rice has dissolved into the milk and the mixture is creamy.

4. Remove from the heat and either serve hot or leave to cool. Serve in bowls topped with the almond and pistachio slices.

Gulab jamun

Deep-fried dumplings in syrup

One of the most famous sweet recipes in Asian homes, these deep-fried dumplings dipped in cardamom syrup are a beloved celebratory dessert and no Indian celebration is complete without them. Simply prepare a batch ahead of time and serve it to your family and dinner guests with a scoop of ice cream or a cup of masala chai (see page 69).

MAKES 10

100g unsweetened milk
  powder, sifted
60g plain flour
½ tsp baking powder
2 tbsp ghee or clarified butter,
  at room temperature
4 tbsp milk, plus 2 tbsp extra
  for the dough
vegetable oil, for deep frying

FOR THE SYRUP

450g caster sugar
500ml water
2 green cardamom pods,
  opened slightly
¼ tsp saffron threads
1 tsp lemon juice

1. Place the milk powder, flour and baking powder in a mixing bowl. Add the ghee and mix with your hands until the mixture forms a light crumbly dough.

2. Add the milk and bring the mixture together – you might need another 2 tablespoons to create a wet dough. Bring the dough together using your fingertips to squeeze and firm it into a ball. Try not to knead the dough as this can create a hard *gulab jamun*. Allow to rest for 10 minutes while you prepare the sugar syrup.

3. Put the sugar, water, cardamon pods and saffron into a large saucepan. Stir and bring to a simmer, and cook on a medium heat until it starts to become a thick syrup. Add the lemon juice and remove the pan from the heat.

4. Pour vegetable oil into a deep saucepan until it is three- quarters full. Heat the oil on a high heat until it reaches 180°C. If you don't have a thermometer you can test the heat by dropping some of the batter into the oil – if it is ready the batter will rise with a sizzle. Grease your hands with some oil and use a tablespoon to spoon out equal amounts of dough and form it into balls by rolling it in your hands until smooth.

5. Gently slide the balls into the hot oil using a slotted spoon, frying them in batches without overcrowding the pan. Reduce the heat to low and continuously turn the balls, using the slotted spoon, trying not to break them. When they change from a light to a dark brown they are ready to be taken out.

CONTINUES OVERLEAF →

6. Remove the balls using the slotted spoon and drain on kitchen paper then place them straight into the syrup. Mix well and allow the *gulab jamuns* to soak up the syrup for at least 2–3 hours or overnight. You will notice that the balls double in size.

7. Serve warm with ice cream or enjoy with tea. You can reheat the *gulab jamuns* in the microwave with syrup for 30 seconds (any longer than this and they becomehard), or gently over a low–medium heat in a small pan.

8. Store any leftover balls and syrup in an airtight container in the fridge for up to 3 days. Ensure the balls are fully submerged in the syrup to prevent them turning hard. You can also freeze the cooked balls in the syrup for up to 3 months in a freezable container. Simply defrost the whole container before reheating and eating.

Kulfi

Kulfi is a rich, nutty spiced ice cream. It is a popular dessert that is surprisingly simple to make with everyday cupboard ingredients. Whenever I eat kulfi, I'm transported back to India where I first fell in love with this street food and tried every possible flavour. Growing up, kulfi was our go-to dessert, and Mum would always have some on hand in the freezer. In my opinion, nothing makes dinner feel more festive than serving guests this traditional aromatic home-made ice cream.

MAKES 6–8

750ml whole milk,
    plus an extra 3 tbsp
15g unsalted pistachios
15g almonds
1 tbsp cornflour
80g evaporated milk
2½ tbsp granulated sugar
6 green cardamom pods

YOU WILL ALSO NEED

6–8 kulfi moulds (I use my
    mum's traditional silver
    ones that are 6cm in
    height) or 1–2 large-square
    ice-cube trays

1. Add the 750ml of milk to a wide, deep saucepan and heat over a low heat for 15 minutes, stirring as it thickens to avoid it burning at the bottom of the pan.

2. While this is cooking, prepare the rest of the ingredients. Open the cardamom pods and grind the seeds to a powder using a pestle and mortar.

3. Blitz the nuts coarsely using a food processor or chop them by hand using a sharp knife – be sure to ensure they still have crunch and are not a powder.

4. Whisk the cornflour with the 3 tablespoons of milk in a bowl, ensuring there are no lumps.

5. Add the sugar to the milk pan and cook, stirring, until dissolved. After 3–4 minutes add the cornflour paste and keep stirring with a spatula as the milk thickens. Keep stirring to remove any lumps as the consistency thickens, and scrape down the sides of the pan.

6. Add the evaporated milk, ground cardamom and nuts to the pan and cook for a further 2–3 minutes until the mixture thickens to a thick custard consistency. Remove from the heat and taste to check the sweetness, adding more sugar or cardamom if desired.

CONTINUED →

7. Allow to cool then transfer the mixture to the kulfi moulds or the ice-cube trays. Freeze overnight or for 12 hours, until the kulfi is firm.

8. Before serving, bring back to room temperature to allow the kulfi to slide out of the moulds easily, or carefully place the moulds under a hot tap. If you have used an ice-cube tray, allow it to defrost a little or run a hot knife around the sides of each cube.

Drinks

Masala chai

Sipping a warm cup of masala chai reminds me of peaceful Sunday mornings spent preparing a traditional Indian brunch with my family It makes me feel nostalgic and evokes comfort. The ritual of brewing the spiced tea feels almost meditative, and the first sip is utterly soothing as the warmth of the aromatic spices envelops you. Let it become a moment of pause and reflection in your day and make an extra batch of the spice blend to share with loved ones. This is my mother's cherished recipe.

SERVES 2

400ml water
1 tsp masala chai mix
  (see below)
2 x black teabags
  (I use an everyday tea,
  such as Tetley or PG Tips)
milk of choice
sugar or sweetener, to taste

FOR THE MASALA CHAI MIX

50g ground ginger
50g green cardamom
1 large cinnamon stick
  or 15g ground cinnamon
30g black peppercorns
8g whole cloves
2g ground nutmeg

1. In a spice grinder, combine all the spices for the masala chai mix and grind to a fine powder. Pause halfway through to stir the spices and ensure they are properly ground.

2. To make sure there aren't any pieces left in the chai mix, sift it into a bowl. Place the mix in a clean, airtight container. It will keep well for 6–12 months.

3. To make the tea, heat the water in a saucepan over a low heat and add the masala chai mix and teabags before the liquid starts to boil and allow them to infuse for at least 2–3 minutes.

4. Stir in the milk and bring to a boil; this is when the chai begins to foam up really fast so keep a close eye on it. If you would like a stronger tea taste, allow the liquid to boil for 5–10 minutes.

5. Remove the teabags, add sugar to taste, and strain into mugs.

Spiced spritzer

The vibrant hues of this spiced spritzer mocktail make it a showstopper.
The blend of aromatic spices accentuates the natural flavours of the fruit
juices It's a sophisticated mocktail that will make guests feel special and
allow you to mark the festivities in style.

MAKES 1

1 whole clove
1 star anise, crushed into
    2–3 pieces
1 tsp pomegranate seeds
15ml cranberry juice
15ml orange juice
pink lemonade or non-
    alcoholic sparkling wine,
    to taste
1 small cinnamon stick,
    crushed into 2–3 pieces

1. Place the crushed spices and pomegranate
   seeds in a coupe or martini glass.

2. Add the cranberry and orange juices, then top
   with your sparkling drink of choice. Mix with
   the pieces of cinnamon and serve.

Cucumber mint cooler

A simple, refreshing mocktail that will be a hit for Diwali.
It is aromatic with savoury and sweet notes that mix well together.

SERVES 4

1 large cucumber, peeled and
   sliced, plus 1 optional extra
   cucumber shaved into
   ribbons to garnish
20g mint leaves, plus extra
   leaves to garnish
juice of 1 lime
1 tsp black salt or table salt
1 x 330ml can of lemonade
lemon slices, to garnish

1. Place the cucumber in a blender with the mint.
   Blitz to a pulp and then push it through a fine
   sieve to strain as much juice as you can – you
   may need to do this twice to get a very smooth
   liquid. You can do this part ahead of time.

2. Divide the juice between 4 small tumblers, then
   add the lime juice and black salt. Put some ice in
   the tumblers and top up with lemonade. Garnish
   with lemon slices, the cucumber ribbons and
   mint leaves and serve immediately.

Apple, elderflower and mint sparkle

This effervescent mocktail captures the essence of summer but can be enjoyed all year around. You can make the base of this drink ahead of time and simply top up with sparkling water or soda when your guests arrive.

SERVES 8-10

1 litre cloudy apple juice
75ml elderflower cordial
handful of mint leaves,
    roughly chopped, plus
    a few leaves to garnish
1 lime, sliced
1 large green apple, cored
    and sliced
1 litre soda or sparkling water.
ice for serving

1. Add the apple juice, elderflower cordial and mint leaves to a large jug. Mix well before adding in the limes and apple slices and set aside to allow the flavours to develop.

2. To serve, put some ice into a tall tumbler and pour over the fruit juice mixture, including some of the fruit, to about halfway up the sides.

3. Finish by topping up the glass with soda or sparkling water. Garnish with extra mint leaves before serving.

Festive ice cubes

Take your Diwali drinks to the next level with these festive spiced ice cubes that will add a touch of elegance to your dinner parties. Guests will admire this beautiful decorative ice while they sip their joyful drinks. Be sure to make these a night before Diwali to have them ready for the celebrations.

**FILLS 1 STANDARD
ICE-CUBE TRAY**

2 oranges, very thinly sliced
½ tsp pomegranate seeds
    per cube
1 whole clove for each ice cube
5 star anise, each broken into
    2 pieces
80ml cranberry juice

1. Have ready a standard ice-cube tray. Cut each orange slice in half to create half moons, then fold each piece to fit into each cube. The orange slices will come out taller than the ice cube, but this is the effect you are after. Scatter over the pomegranate seeds, and add 1 clove to each cube.

2. Add a star anise piece to each cube, then carefully pour some cranberry juice into each cube to come halfway up. Top up with some water and leave to freeze for 8 hours or overnight.

Serving food in a thali

In Indian culture, meals are an offering, and how we arrange dishes carries meaning. Hindus pray with gratitude before eating, and specific prayers connect us to the divine act of nourishing our bodies and souls.

The thali represents this holistic approach to dining. A thali is a large circular rimmed plate that holds smaller bowls (known as *katoris* in Hindi) filled with a variety of different wet and dry curries. With its array of small dishes, a thali provides a balanced meal of carbohydrates, protein, fats and fibre, as well as diverse flavours and textures, which aligns with the Hindu Ayurvedic philosophy of nourishing the body and mind.

Each component of the thali carries significance, creating a sensory and spiritual experience. More than just a meal, this style of dining celebrates our heritage and focus on holistic nourishment. When we dine from a thali, we tune in to the wisdom of generations past, appreciating the joy and mindfulness that traditional foods can bring.

A thali platter also symbolises life's abundance: flavours intermixing like varied human experiences, and there is a right way to place dishes purposefully, to allow this synergy. Sweet accompanies sour, soft tempers hard, spicy sits alongside mild. Opposites balance to craft harmony.

What should be included in a thali?

In a traditional thali, the different curries and sauces are placed around the sides with a heap of rice positioned in the centre. Each of the curries and sauces is mixed with the rice one at a time and eaten in a specific order. You begin by eating any of the vegetables, both dry and wet, and then would add the wet dal (different variations) to rice. Traditionally a thali is eaten with your hands, but you can use a spoon for the rice. You use the yoghurt to help cool your palate; it also helps with digestion and balances out the chutneys and hot food. Finish with your dessert. This is just a guide, so enjoy with your heart – it is a fun way to enjoy a wholesome meal experience.

The image below suggests how to arrange a traditional thali. Take inspiration from customary traditions and heritage when arranging your next meal.

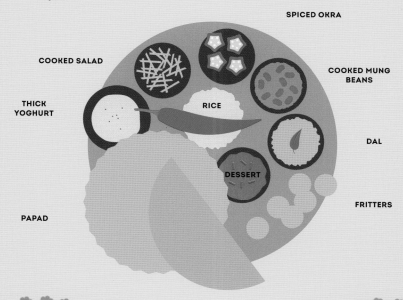

SPICED OKRA

COOKED SALAD

COOKED MUNG BEANS

THICK YOGHURT

RICE

DAL

DESSERT

PAPAD

FRITTERS

ROTI/NAAN

CHAPTER 02

Crafts

Crafts

As parents know, crafting and creating alongside children fosters precious bonding while making lasting memories. Diwali offers many opportunities for such creative connections through projects that also add meaning and magic to your celebrations. This chapter provides ideas for thoughtful crafts that families can enjoy in the lead up to the festival of lights.

Light welcomes the goddess Lakshmi, while symbolising her guidance and goodness entering our lives. The decorations and projects you'll find in this chapter are beautiful ways families can welcome Lakshmi's divine presence, usher in blessings and prepare for a new year filled with light.

Craft salt dough *diya* lamps; make simple rangoli stencils or flower garlands, and watch children beam with pride when they display their handicrafts and feel connected to your Diwali traditions.

Diyas

Salt dough candle holders

Making salt dough candle holders is a fun and inexpensive craft for kids. Follow this recipe to create colourful and magical Diwali candle holders that may be enjoyed year after year. You will need to begin this craft a few days before your Diwali celebrations to allow the dough and paint time to dry thoroughly.

MAKES 6–8 (DEPENDING ON SIZE)

1 cup plain flour (do not use self-raising flour as it will rise during baking)
½ cup table salt
½ cup water

EQUIPMENT

measuring cup
medium mixing bowl
whisk or spoon
baking paper or silicone baking mat
baking tray

DECORATE WITH

acrylic paint suitable for clay
glitter
gems
sequins

YOU WILL ALSO NEED

tealights

1. Find a workspace where you can create a little bit of a mess. Have all the equipment to hand. and measure out the ingredients before you begin.

2. In a medium mixing bowl, stir together the flour and salt. Gradually add the water while stirring the flour and salt mixture until it is fully combined and smooth.

3. Remove the dough from the mixing bowl and knead it for 5 minutes, then let it rest for 15 minutes. Add a little flour if the dough is too sticky or a few drops of water if it is too dry – the dough should resemble clay.

4. Meanwhile, preheat the oven to 200°C fan and line a baking sheet with baking paper or a silicone baking mat.

5. Shape the dough into a flat circle then use a knife to cut it into three or four sections, then cut each section in half again. You can make either 6 medium or 8 small *diya* lamps. The dough is really easy to shape using your hands or use the back of a glass to roll it out. You can be extremely creative and shape the *diyas* into traditional teardrops, squares or circular shapes. Before baking, you can squeeze the edges to make a border or pinch a design on them. Just make sure you push down a well in the centre that is big enough to hold your tealight – it's easiest to measure it using a tealight, leaving ample space as the dough will shrink a little as it bakes.

CONTINUES OVERLEAF →

Crafts

CONTINUED →

6. Bake in the oven for 2 hours, until dry and hard, then remove and allow to cool completely. Let your *diyas* air-dry for a couple of days to ensure they are completely dry before you paint them, turning them over every now and again so that the bottoms dry too.

7. Paint your diyas and let them dry for 3–4 hours. Using a fine brush you can add some pretty detail. Alternatively, try adding some sparkle with sequins, gems and glitter; you can use a glue gun for this.

8. Once your decorations have dried, place tealights inside your holders and light the candles. Place at windowsills or entryways to bring light into your home. Place a candle tray under your *diyas*, to avoid any colour marking white painted surfaces and never leave lit candles unattended.

Marigold flower garland

These stunning paper marigolds will brighten up your home. This is a beautiful craft you can enjoy with the help of your little ones and the garlands can be used for all festivities. I've suggested using a mixture of yellow and orange flowers, but you could use a single colour if you prefer. You can also create bigger flowers by cutting out larger squares or adding more sheets of paper.

MAKES 1 GARLAND (AROUND 20 FLOWERS)

6 sheets of orange tissue paper (75 x 50cm) or 3 sheets of yellow and 3 of orange
thin string
scissors
glue gun or glue dot stickers
ruler or measuring tape.
1–1.2m length of ribbon (about 1.5–2cm wide) to stick the garlands to, depending on how long you would like to make the garland
4 large paper clips
pencil

1. Stack six pieces of tissue papers. If you want to create a two-tone flower, layer 3 sheets of yellow and 3 sheets of orange alternating each colour.

2. Using the paper clips to hold the paper together, mark out 15 x 10cm rectangles on the sheet with the pencil, then cut out rectangles in columns, trying to keep all the sheets together.

3. Take one group of 6 sheets and with the shortest side of the paper facing you, make a 1cm fold, then keep folding, going back and forth to create a fan (see page 90).

4. Secure the folds by carefully tying them with string around the middle. The fastening should be tight.

5. Unfold each side to create a bow shape. Holding the centre, carefully pull the first layer of paper up towards you, then repeat with all the sheets on one side of the fan before doing the same with the other half of the fan.

6. Gently fluff out the layers of the flower to create some texture and volume.

7. Once you have created your desired number of flowers, depending on how big you would like your garland, place the ribbon flat on a large surface and as a quick measurement place the flowers along it so you can see how many you will need.

8. Put a little bit of glue on the back of the flower and press it firmly on to the ribbon. Continue until you have filled your length.

9. Allow to dry for 1-2 hours before securing the ends of the ribbon together and hanging.

Diwali poster templates

Here I've included three Diwali poster templates from which you and your children can create Diwali posters. Simply trace the outline templates then let the children's creativity run wild as they colour and personalise their designs. Seeing their homemade posters up during Diwali will fill your children with pride and excitement for the celebrations.

tracing paper
paper clips
pencil
rubber
stiff paper
colouring pencils
    or felt tips

1. Place your tracing paper over the poster design and secure the paper with paper clips to keep it straight.

2. Take a pencil and carefully draw over the outline of the poster template.

3. Remove the paper clips and place the tracing paper on a new sheet of plain paper for your poster, again keeping it in place with paper clips.

4. Using the pencil, trace over the outline of the tracing paper shape, applying a little pressure so that the design comes through on to the plain paper.

5. Remove the paper clips and you should see the template outline ready for you to colour. Using your choice of colouring tools enjoy creating a beautiful Diwali poster.

Orange candles

This is a beautiful, DIY candle idea that leaves a fresh natural aroma in your home for a puja and makes a striking decoration on your Diwali table.

large oranges
sharp knife
chopping board
cotton wicks
chopsticks/lollypop sticks
   to keep the wick in place
bay leaves or cinnamon sticks
   (optional)
plate/tray to keep
   the orange on
coconut oil

1. Carefully, slice the orange horizontally through its middle and carefully scoop out the inside (save this to avoid food waste). Try not to rip the skin as this will be the base for the candle holder.

2. Position a cotton wick at the bottom, using chopsticks to hold it in place.

3. If you are using them, place the bay leaves or some cinnamon sticks inside the orange shell; you might need to break them up so that they fit neatly in the space around the wick.

4. Place the orange shells on a plate or tray. Melt some coconut oil in a small pan over a low heat and carefully pour it into the orange shell, filling three quarters of the shell.

5. Allow the oil to cool – it will solidify and harden as it cools.

6. Carefully light your candles during the puja, placing a tray or a plate underneath them to catch any spillages. Never leave a burning candle unattended.

Rangoli paper quilling

One of the most iconic decorations of Diwali is rangoli, the vibrant art patterns meticulously created to decorate entrances and floors. Rangoli designs are crafted from materials like coloured rice, dried flower petals, coloured sand, chalk and, as here, quilled paper. Traditional motifs include geometric shapes, floral patterns and spiritual symbols associated with divinity: swirls, lines, and dots interweave to form stunning designs bursting with auspicious meaning. During Diwali, rangoli designs often incorporate *diyas*. The elaborate creative process of rangoli embodies welcoming Lakshmi into homes. Rangoli adds a dynamic visual dimension to Diwali decor. This beautiful activity enables you to spend quality time with your children while practising a mindful craft.

piece of paper or card on to which to stick the quills
paper quilling strips in different colours (these are available in most sizes either online or at a craft store – or you can shred your own paper at home)
quilling tool (not essential, you can also use a toothpick, or a pencil or crayons for bigger patterns)
paper glue
brush for the glue
scissors

1. Draw the design you want to create on to a piece of paper or card, such as a flower or traditional teardrop rangoli shape.

2. Now start to roll the quilling paper around your chosen tool to make tight rolls (see page 100): make a tiny fold at one end of the paper and roll it all the way to the end. You can keep some rolls tight for any detailed patterns you are going to design, or you can make some loose rolls by allowing the paper to unroll slightly. Add a tiny dot of glue to the end of the paper to secure it.

3. You can create round, teardrop or diamond shapes. To make a teardrop shape, roll up a tight quill. Squeeze one side and mark a fold in the paper to create the tip, then slightly loosen the other end. Secure it with a dot of glue and your shape is ready. To make a diamond shape, squeeze both sides. Glue the open end to secure the shape.

4. To make your paper quills bigger or more colourful you can glue a strip of a different colour to the first and roll it in the same way.

5. Create as many rolls as you think you need to fill your design on the paper or card. I would suggest having most of your shapes ready ahead of gluing as this will give you a better indication of the number of coils you require.

CONTINUED →

6. Once you have positioned enough coils on the page to create your design, using a brush, brush the glue on to each coil and gently press it on to the paper.

7. Once you have made your rangoli pattern, allow it to dry. You can also frame your pattern after Diwali or create patterns on smaller pieces of folded paper to create your own Diwali cards.

Diwali lanterns

Crafting Diwali lanterns is a wonderful way to add warmth and ambiance to your celebrations. These hand-made lanterns can serve as stunning centrepieces, welcoming entrance decorations, or thoughtful gifts for family and friends. Decorate them with rhinestones, sequins, or with a beautiful statement ribbon.

heatproof glass jars
    or Mason jars
small candles or tealights
plain paper
Sellotape or Blu-tack
all-purpose spray paint
    in different colours
old newspaper
paint pens
foam brush
glue (all purpose, craft glue
    for glass)
glitter or any other
    embellishments, such as
    colourful gems, sequins
    or rhinestones
large bowl
ribbons (optional)

1. If you are using old jars with sticky labels on them, be sure to wash the jars thoroughly by boiling them in water, then remove the label and dry the jars carefully.

2. To make a window for the tealight, cut out a 7cm circle from the plain paper for each jar and stick it in the same place on each one using a rolled up piece of Sellotape or Blu-tack.

3. If you are spray painting the jar, protect your workspace with newspaper. Spray your glass lanterns in different bright colours. Spray over the paper circle too. Leave to dry for 3-4 hours.

4. Once dry, if you are going for a glitter effect, use your foam brush to cover the jar in glue, but do not cover the bottom. Place the jar in the large bowl, spoon the glitter over the glue and leave to dry.

5. Once dry, remove the paper circle and add any other decorations, such as sequins or gems using the glue gun, or other details using the paint pens. If using a ribbon, tie it around the rim of the jar.

6. Place a candle or tealight in the jar and light. Remember, never leave a burning candle unattended.

Diwali tealight candles

This is a simple and aesthetically pleasing way to decorate candles with vibrant designs and auspicious symbols to use as meaningful Diwali gifts and table decorations.

MAKES 12

lint free cloth
12 unscented tealight candles
    (you can use a mixture
    of sizes)
coloured acrylic paint
    (see Tip below)
    or pens
thin paint brushes
    (if using paint)
gems (optional)

1. Using a lint free cloth clean the tealight surface to remove any dust or pieces of wax.

2. Paint your design straight on to the candle using a paint brush or pen. You can create any design or symbol – use the picture opposite for inspiration. You can always practise on paper first or use a stencil.

3. Let the first coat of paint dry before applying a second coat, if required. The number of coats you need will be determined by the colour of the paint and the design. Often one is enough.

4. Leave to dry for 2 hours.

5. Once the candles are finished, handle with care as the paint can chip or scratch easily.

6. Place in an organza bag or decorated box to gift (see page 154 for ideas on how to present and package gifts).

TIP

Please note it's important to use acrylic paint to paint your candles. Acrylic paint is safe to use on candles so long as you use non-toxic, water-based acrylic paint. Rememer never to leave a lit flame unattended.

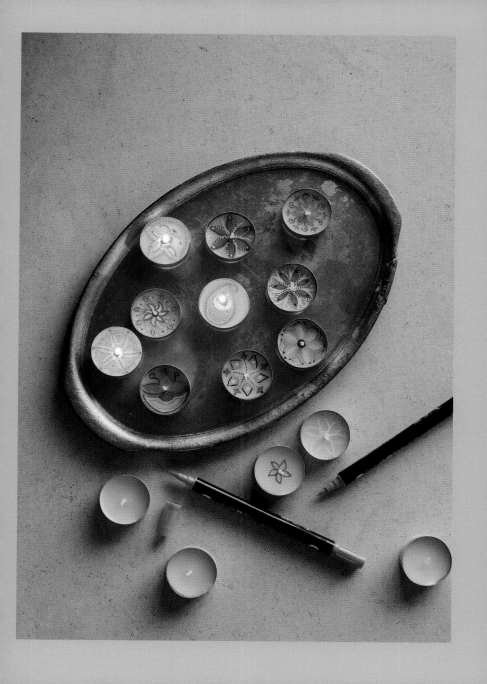

Paper plate Diwali lamps

This simple craft allows kids to get creative and hands-on in your Diwali preparations. You can use the paper lamps to decorate windowsills, create bunting by making several paper lights and tying them together with string, or why not use the lamps as a Diwali card?

plain round white paper plates
paint or crayons
paper glue
coloured paper in red, yellow and orange
glitter, any other embellishments, such as gems or sequins

1. Fold a paper plate in half to create a crescent shape.

2. Decorate your plate by painting it or colouring it in with crayons. If you are painting, then allow the paint to dry before you start to decorate (for speed, paint just 1 layer).

3. Draw a flame shape on to each sheet of coloured paper in 3 different sizes, with red being the largest shape, then orange and yellow to provide an ombre flame (see opposite). Or use the templates on pages 168 and 169 to trace them on to your paper.

4. Glue the flame layers together starting with the largest and layer them so that all three can be seen. Then glue this along the straight side in the middle of the plate so it looks like it is flickering.

5. Finish by sticking on any glitter and other embellishments.

Rangoli sand

Rangoli are beautiful patterns created on the floor or a tabletop and they can be made from a variety of materials, among them sand. Their purpose is more than decoration; they are intended to express happiness and positivity and are designed to welcome the goddess of wealth and luck, Lakshmi, into the home, as well as to keep evil at bay. There are many rangoli stencils in traditional shapes and designs available online to help you create colourful patterns from sand. To make this craft easier, I recommend purchasing one.

coloured sand (in various colours)
small jars, pots or bowls
large tray
white or black paper
rangoli stencils (optional)
zip seal bags

1. Line the tray with paper. You can either work your sand freehand (or use a stencil, which makes it a lot easier and faster to plan out the design).

2. Pour small amounts of each coloured sand into little bowls.

3. If using a stencil, use a teaspoon to scoop out your first sand colour and carefully cover one part of the stencil panel, then, in no particular order, fill the other panels, using other colours to create a pretty mixture. Alternatively, you can just add the sand to the tray and mark out your design with a spoon or your fingers.

4. Continue to use different colours to create a pattern and fill out the stencil, then very gently and carefully lift the stencil away.

5. Keep the pattern in the tray for as long as you wish, then scoop the sand into zip seal bags to create a multicoloured design another time.

Flower tealight holders

Embrace the spirit of sustainability by transforming humble kitchen roll tubes into unique and charming tealight holders.

3–4 kitchen paper tubes, depending on how many holders you want to make
scissors
1 x thin and 1 x thick paint brush
coloured paints
glitter pen
stickers, to decorate

1. Use scissors to cut the kitchen paper tubes in half, then in half again to make four equal-sized pieces.

2. Make four equal cuts down the length of the holders, but not going all the way to the end (leave roughly the height of a tealight).

3. Fold each cut section of the tube down to create the petals of a flower shape. You can also create different shapes by making 5 or 6 petals, and shaping them too (see opposite).

4. Once you have cut your shapes, paint the holders in different colours, ensuring to paint the inside and bottom too.

5. Allow to dry before painting a second coat.

6. Once dry you can add some details using glitter pens, or a different-coloured paint using the thin paint brush. When this layer is dry add your tealight and gift this to family or friends. Before lighting, place the holder on a coaster and ensure the 'petals' are away from the flame. Remember never to leave a lit candle unattended

CHAPTER 03

Gifts

Gifts

Gifting holds deep cultural significance during Diwali. Exchanging thoughtful gifts creates a generous heart, strengthens friendships and conveys blessings for prosperity. Traditionally, common Diwali gifts include gold, silver, sweets, clothing, decorative items and *diyas*. New items signify new beginnings associated with the new year. Gifts are elaborately wrapped and presented to loved ones.

Offering edible gifts is a meaningful Diwali tradition. Handmade sweets or savoury snacks show loved ones how much you care by giving something personal in which you've invested time and love. This chapter contains are a few easy ideas that you can make ahead of the festival, as well as ways you can personalise your gifts through homemade wrapping and handmade cards.

Diwali presents encourage us to be compassionate in all of our interactions and the essence of the festival is brought to life through selfless giving and gracious receiving.

Felt stamps and handmade wrapping paper

This is a cute and enjoyable activity to allow you to customise your Diwali gifts, making them special and one of a kind. You can create a variety of shapes and patterns for your stamps.

sponge or large piece of thick felt (about 3cm thick)
felt-tip pen
glue/glue gun
craft paint
thick cardboard (from an old box rather than a cereal box)
scissors
gold or silver pen
thin paint brush
any decorative gems, sequins, or glitter,
brown kraft or white paper, to print on

1. Cut a 7 x 7cm square from the sponge or felt.

2. Draw a decorative shape on to the felt (use the templates on pages 167 and 168 as a guide for traditional Diwali shapes, or create your own design). Cut out the shape and any holes within the shape. You can make more than one for the wrapping paper.

3. Cut out a cardboard square a centimetre or two larger than the stamp. Apply some glue to the felt, stick it to the cardboard and allow this to dry for 10–15 minutes.

4. Spread the brown kraft paper out – if it is on a roll, weigh down the corners.

5. Squeeze some paint into a saucer, dip the stamp in the paint and start printing. Create a pattern, and once dry finish with some glitter, or outline the designs with a gold or silver pen. You can also use the stamps to create personalised gift tags or greetings cards.

Trinket boxes

Trinket boxes are an excellent keepsake. Create these beautiful, adorned gifts to give to family and friends on Diwali by upcycling old tins or small jars. You can make them extra special by personalising them.

small tins or old jars with lids
metal paint (for tins) and/or
     acrylic paint (for glass)
paint brush
glue gun
gems, glitter, pearls
     and letter stickers
     (for personalisation)
ribbon (optional)

1. Wash and dry your tins and jars.

2. Paint the tins or jars – you may need a few layers depending on the material. Allow to dry between each layer.

3. Once dry embellish with gems, pearls, glitter or letter stickers and wrap your tin or jar with a pretty ribbon if you are gifting them.

Make your own gift tags and Diwali cards

These gift tags allow you to personalise presents for loved ones in a meaningful way. You can also use them as decorative thank you notes or place name cards for Diwali gatherings. I've included customised Diwali templates ready for you to copy. Simply colour the motifs, add your own messages and attach the tags to your wrapped gifts. The variety of designs means you can pick different ones for each recipient. I hope these gift tags inspire you to make your festive gifts a little more heartfelt!

tracing paper
paper clips
pencil
rubber
plain or coloured paper
colouring pencils or felt tips
scissors
string or colourful ribbon
    to feed through the tag
    (optional)

1. Place your tracing paper over the gift tag template (see pages 124–127) and secure the paper with paper clips to keep it straight.

2. Take a pencil and carefully draw over the outline of the tag design.

3. Remove the paperclips and place the tracing paper on a new sheet of paper for your tag, again keeping it in place with paper clips.

4. Using the pencil, trace over the outline of the tracing paper shape, applying a little pressure so that the design comes through on to the paper.

5. Remove the paperclips and paper; you should see the outline ready for you to colour. Using your choice of pencils or felt tips, enjoy creating a gift tag.

6. Cut a hole in the top of the gift tag and thread through some string or a ribbon (or leave the card plain if you're just making a place name card).

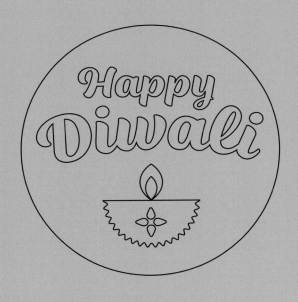

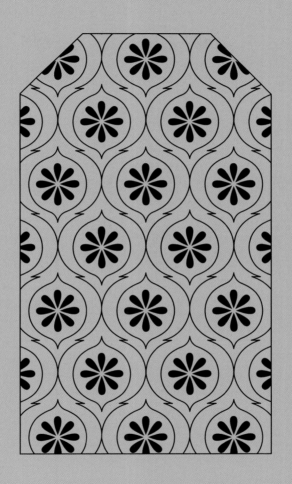

Edible gift ideas

Masala nuts

A beloved Diwali gift-giving tradition is artfully packaging crunchy spiced nuts. By coating almonds, cashews, peanuts and pecans in a blend of mouth-watering spices then roasting them to perfection, masala nuts become a craveable snack – their aromatic heat combined with the crunch makes them hard to stop eating once you start. Beautifully packed in festive bags or jars, masala nuts convey wishes for prosperity and health in the new year. You can also set out bowls of nuts for guests to enjoy throughout the celebrations. I know these will be a hit at Diwali.

**MAKES 260G
(ABOUT 3 SMALL JARS)**

120g almonds
75g cashews
30g peanuts
30g pecans
2 tbsp olive oil
1 tbsp gram flour (besan)
1 tbsp cornflour
1 tbsp rice flour (if you don't
    have all three just double
    up on the one you have but
    try and add gram flour)

FOR THE MASALA SPICE MIX

1 tsp ground turmeric
1 tsp kala namak
1 tsp smoked paprika
1 tsp chilli powder
1 tsp ground cumin
1 tsp ground coriander
1 tsp garam masala
1 tsp chaat masala, plus extra
    to finish
1 tsp citric acid
1 tsp sea salt

1. Preheat the oven to 180°C fan. Line a baking tray with baking paper.

2. Add all the nuts to a bowl with the spice mix, then add the oil and mix well.

3. Mix in the flours, which should coat and stick to the nuts, then spread the nuts out on the lined tray (you may need to roast them in batches).

4. Roast in the oven for 15 minutes, until golden brown. Stir and turn them from time to time as some nuts cook faster and brown quicker.

5. Remove from the oven and leave to cool, then sprinkle with some chaat masala before serving and storing in clean glass jars!

Edible gift ideas

Nankhatai

Almond cookies

Buttery almond *nankhatai* have graced Indian celebrations for generations, as they come together from store-cupboard ingredients with little fuss. My *nankhatai* recipe has been perfected over years of observing my family make them. The cookies are best served with a hot cup of chai (see page 69).

MAKES 18 SMALL COOKIES

175g plain flour
25g fine semolina
pinch of salt
7-8 green cardamoms
¼ tsp ground nutmeg
115g ghee, at room temperature
80g caster sugar
¼ tsp almond extract
2 tbsp slivered pistachios or almonds

1. Line two large baking trays with baking paper.

2. Sift the flour into a large bowl, then add the semolina, salt, cardamom and nutmeg.

3. In a separate bowl, whisk the ghee and sugar for 5 minutes until light and creamy. Add this to the flour mixture, along with the almond extract and use a spatula to gently fold the mixture together. If the dough is looking dry, add another teaspoon of ghee and lightly mix until it comes together as a cookie dough.

4. Cover the dough with cling film and refrigerate for 30 minutes.

5. Remove from the fridge and grease your hands with a little ghee. Take 1 tablespoon of the mixture and roll it in your hands to form a smooth ball, then flatten it slightly. Place on the lined tray and repeat with the remaining mixture, leaving a 1-2cm gap between each cookie as they will expand during baking.

6. Cover the trays with cling film and refrigerate for 20 minutes. Preheat the oven to 190°C fan.

7. Lift off the cling film and scatter the nuts on top of the cookies. Bake for 15 minutes. Check them regularly as this time approaches so that you don't over-bake them – when they're ready the edges will be firm and slightly golden with a soft filling. Remove from the oven and allow to cool. They will firm up as they cool.

8. Once cool, place in an airtight container and enjoy with chai. The cookies can be kept for 7–10 days, but I doubt they will last that long!

Coconut ladoo

Ladoo are known as the 'king of sweets' and are a famous Indian treat traditionally made of flour, sugar and ghee. The circular shape symbolises wealth, while the sweetness is a blessing for a sweet life ahead. There are numerous kinds of *ladoo* but coconut *ladoo* plays a specific role in Diwali celebrations due to the coconut's meaning: in Hindu tradition coconuts are associated with purity, prosperity and fertility. My simple coconut *ladoo* are a quick sweet treat to make for Diwali or other Indian festivities.

MAKES 10

200g desiccated coconut
165g condensed milk
¼ tsp ground cardamom
   (optional, but highly
   recommended)
granulated sugar,
   to decorate (optional)
pistachios or almonds,
   halved, to decorate
   (optional)

1. Add the desiccated coconut to a small frying pan set over a medium heat. Lightly toast the coconut, stirring frequently, until it just begins to brown. At this point, take the pan off the heat and immediately transfer the coconut to a medium-sized mixing bowl. Remove and set aside 3 tablespoons.

2. Add roughly three quarters of the condensed milk and the ground cardamom, if using, to the remaining coconut in the bowl, and stir with a spatula until well combined; you are aiming for a mixture which is slightly sticky – test it by seeing if the mixture holds together in a ball. Adjust the consistency by adding more condensed milk or some of the reserved coconut until you can easily handle the mixture.

3. Take 1 tablespoon of the mixture and roll it into a ball using your hands.

4. You can enjoy the *ladoo* as they are, or decorate them by gently rolling them in sugar or some of the reserved coconut and topping them with halved pistachios or almonds.

5. Store the *ladoo* in an airtight container in the fridge for up to 7 days.

Easy barfi

Barfi is a traditional sweet made during Diwali and its presence
is associated with joyful moments, festivals and religious ceremonies.
No celebration is complete without *barfi* or other Indian sweets (*mithais*)
as they represent celebration, happiness, good omens and prosperity.
This fudgy *barfi* milk confection is one of the simplest yet most cherished.

MAKES 16

330g whole milk powder
165g caster sugar
250ml whole milk
60g ghee
3 tbsp pistachios or almonds,
    roughly chopped
edible rose petals, to
    decorate (optional)

1. Line a 16cm square baking tin with baking paper.

2. In a bowl, whisk together the milk powder, sugar and milk until they are well combined and there are no lumps.

3. Transfer the mixture to a non-stick saucepan and add the ghee.

4. Cook over a low heat, mixing and stirring continuously, until the mixture thickens and starts to come together. This takes about 10 minutes at which point you will notice it will start to pull away from the sides of the pan.

5. Remove from the heat and spread the mixture evenly into the lined tray. Use a spatula to press it down firmly.

6. Top with the pistachios or almonds and gently press them in.

7. Refrigerate for 1–2 hours or until completely set.

8. Cut the set *barfi* into 16 squares, and scatter with the rose petals if serving, otherwise store in an airtight container in the fridge for up to 7 days.

Chocolate dates

Chocolate-covered dates are easy, impressive edible gifts and treats to enjoy for Diwali. Making a batch is sure to delight – both in the creative process and in the resulting decadent flavours. They are perfect for gifting to friends and family in pretty packages and you can also arrange them on platters alongside other sweets to serve guests. Their blend of sticky-sweet fruit makes them hard to resist!

MAKES 40

40 Medjool dates
100g pistachios
100g salted almonds
100g roasted peanuts
3 pinches of ground
   cardamom or cinnamon
100g dark chocolate,
   chopped
50g milk chocolate chips
25g white chocolate chips

1. Use a sharp knife to make an incision along each date and remove the stone.

2. Stuff one type of nut into each date, closing up the date around the nuts so they're completely hidden – it's important not to over-stuff them so that the date can't close around them.

3. Finely chop the remaining pistachios, almonds and peanuts keeping each type separate. Add a pinch of ground cardamom or cinnamon to each pile of nut. Line 3 baking trays with baking paper.

4. Melt the dark chocolate in a heatproof bowl set over a pan of simmering water without letting the bottom of the bowl touch the water. Once melted, remove from the heat.

5. Dip half the dates in the dark chocolate to coat them completely, then arrange on one of the baking trays. Sprinkle the mixed crushed nuts over most of the dark chocolate dates, choosing a different nut each time to add colour and variety but leaving a few plain for now.

6. Repeat this with the milk chocolate and the remaining nut-stuffed dates, dipping some of these ones only halfway to add visual interest and again leaving a few plain.

7. Finally, melt the white chocolate in the same way and drizzle it over the dates that have not been decorated with nuts.

8. Put the dates in the fridge for 45 minutes to set. Arrange them in a box lined with baking paper and wrap. The dates will keep for up to 2 months, so they are perfect to make ahead of time.

Chocolate and nut coins

These nutty, salty chocolate coins are seriously delicious and make the easiest gift. You can use a variety of toppings, including dried fruit, edible rose petals and different types of nut, and preparing them is a great activity for your little ones too. I like stacking them as a collection of ten and presenting them in a cellophane bag tied with a festive ribbon and a handmade Diwali gift tag (see page 123).

MAKES ABOUT 20 DEPENDING ON THE SIZE OF YOUR CUTTER

100g dark chocolate chips
100g milk chocolate chips
40g white chocolate chips (optional, for drizzling)
50g mixed nuts, half left whole, half chopped
50g dried fruits, such as raisins, apricots and dates, roughly chopped
40g seeds, such as sesame or sunflower seeds
1 tbsp flaky sea salt

YOU WILL ALSO NEED

1 x 5cm round cookie cutter or other round cutters, or you can use silicone muffin moulds

1. Have all your toppings ready in a baking tray so you can easily add them to the coins. Line a separate large baking tray with baking paper or have ready your muffin moulds.

2. Melt the dark chocolate in a heatproof bowl set over a pan of simmering water without letting the bottom of the bowl touch the water.

3. Place your cookie cooker on the lined tray and take 1 tablespoon of chocolate and evenly spread it out in the cookie cutter. Alternatively, spoon the chocolate into the bottom of the muffin mould.

4. Scatter over a mixture of nuts and fruit and finish with a sprinkle of salt, then repeat until you have used up all the chocolate.

5. Repeat this process with the milk chocolate.

6. If you want to decorate the coins using white chocolate you can melt this in a heatproof bowl over a pan of simmering water as with the other chocolate. Use a fork or a teaspoon to drizzle it over some of the coins.

7. Allow the chocolate coins to harden by placing them in the fridge for up to 1 hour. Once cooled you can put them into organza bags or a box for gifting.

8. These keep well in an airtight container at room temperature or in the fridge for up to 1 week.

Rose and pistachio biscuits

These aromatic biscuits offer floral sweetness complemented by nutty richness and each dainty, buttery bite melts on the tongue. Carefully packaging them in decorative tins or boxes makes a meaningful Diwali gift, or you can offer them when hosting celebrations for guests to enjoy them with hot chai (see page 69 for my recipe). However they are shared, these gorgeous biscuits offer a dash of elegance, conveying wishes for an auspicious and sweet new year.

MAKES 6-8

75g pistachios, plus a handful, finely chopped, to decorate
100g rolled oats
100g plain flour
½ tsp bicarbonate of soda
pinch of sea salt
100g unsalted butter
115g caster sugar
1 tsp rose water
½ tsp vanilla extract
edible rose petals

1. Preheat the oven to 180°C fan.

2. Add the pistachios and oats to a blender and pulse for a few seconds to break up the pistachios but leave them chunky.

3. Transfer to a mixing bowl and add the flour, bicarbonate of soda and salt and mix well.

4. In a small saucepan, melt the butter over a low heat, then transfer to a mixing bowl and add the sugar, rose water and vanilla extract. Mix well and add to the oat/flour mixture and mix well again.

5. Take 1½ tablespoons of the mixture and roll it into balls using your hands. I divide the dough first to ensure I have enough for 6-8 biscuits and can make them all the same size. Press each ball down slightly, and scatter over a pinch of the finely chopped pistachios.

6. Place on the lined baking tray, leaving enough space for them to spread as they bake. Bake for 10-12 minutes, until golden brown.

7. Allow to cool then scatter over some rose petals before adding to any gift boxes.

Edible gift ideas

Pistachio barfi truffles

These little balls of chocolate and pistachio deliciousness are inspired by *barfi*. They make a pretty dessert tray as well as a beautiful Diwali gift.

MAKES ABOUT 16-18

60g unsalted butter
6 tbsp whole milk
150g whole milk powder
60gg caster sugar
½ tsp ground cardamom
2 tbsp ground pistachios

TO DECORATE

100g white chocolate
    chips and/or 100g dark
    chocolate chips
crushed pistachios or
    almonds, or desiccated
    coconut, to decorate

1. Line a baking tray with baking paper. In a saucepan over a low heat, melt the butter, then add 4 tablespoons of the milk and stir to combine. Add the milk powder and mix well using a spatula. Cook for 1 minute, until the mixture thickens and forms a loose dough.

2. Add the sugar, cardamom and the remaining milk and cook for a further 2 minutes until you get a soft dough.

3. Add the ground pistachios and on a very low heat continue to mix this dough for 5 minutes until it becomes softer and smoother. It will start to come away from the sides of the pan easily and a pinch of it should feel slightly oily and not stick to your fingers. At this point, remove the pan from the heat, transfer the dough to a plate and flatten it out to cool. Cover with cling film and refrigerate for 30 minutes.

4. Once cool, take tablespoons of the mixture and use your hands to roll it into evenly-sized balls.

5. Melt your chocolate in a heatproof bowl set over a pan of simmering water without letting the bottom of the bowl touch the water. If you are using two different chocolates, do this one at a time in separate bowls.

6. Using two forks dip the balls in the chocolate, and roll around to ensure they are completely covered. Place the truffles on the lined tray. To decorate, dip a teaspoon in the opposite colour chocolate and drizzle it back and forth over the truffle to create lines, then sprinkle with crushed nuts and/or coconut. Allow the truffles to cool and set before transferring them to boxes or gift bags. The truffles can be kept in an airtight container in a cool place for up to 5 days.

CHAPTER 04

Helpful extras

Helpful extras

The Diwali festivities hold deep meaning for Hindus and are eagerly anticipated, but preparing for this elaborate event can at times also feel overwhelming. To offer some additional guidance, this chapter includes a few helpful extras – think of them as my Diwali toolkit to help keep the run-up to the festival calm. Since traditions vary, these tips are intended only to steer your planning, not prescribe it. You'll find a guide to hosting puja and planning your own rituals, and decorating ideas to illuminate your home with festive joy. I've also included my essential Diwali checklist, which keeps me on track. To complete the chapter, I have included the *aarti* lyrics and *Hanuman Chalisa* to give you everything you need for celebrating. I hope that these handy extras will instil a sense of calm, organisation, and light your way as you create your own Diwali traditions with your family.

Decorating your house for Diwali

The creativity and traditions of Diwali fill homes with love and spiritual meaning. Cleaning the house before you start to decorate it is an important element of the preparations and is considered auspicious, as the goddess of wealth – Lakshmi – will visit the house during the festive season.

Next, you will need to purchase materials for the puja (see page 150) as well as Diwali gifts for family and friends. While you can certainly buy gifts, I encourage you to make your own edible gifts, such as homemade *barfi* or chocolate dates (see pages 136 and 139). Getting creative and making gifts adds a more heartfelt touch to the celebrations.

Decorating is the concluding stage in your preparations. Decorate your home with handmade crafts (see pages 81–115), adding many of the decorating ideas opposite too.

Fairy lights

This is a simple, yet impactful way to decorate your house, both inside and out. Twinkling lights are an excellent way to bring atmosphere to any space.

Candles and lanterns

Create a candle display using different heights of candle placed inside hurricane lamps or heatproof vases. Or make your own lanterns (see page 103). Be sure to place a candle in each room and keep the lights on ahead of your Diwali puja as this illuminates the house and brings joy to your home. Place a table outside and arrange candles on trays so that you can welcome your family and guests with a cosy entrance. Please note that lit candles must never be left unattended.

Rangoli designs

Rangoli is an art form in which patterns are created on the floor or a tabletop using a variety of materials. There are auspicious symbols in the patterns, passed from one generation to the next to keep the tradition alive, but rangoli's most important element is to be colourful.

Because Diwali falls in the winter months and rain is frequently forecast in the UK, rangoli would not last outdoors, so placing the designs on a table in your hallway would create a welcoming entrance for guests. Have a look on pages 98 and 110 for different ways to create your own designs using paper quills or sand.

Wall hangings

You can create your own flower garlands (see page 88 for how to make my marigold paper garlands) and use them to make a feature wall, or alternatively, buy simple, colourful wall hangings. Additionally, this will provide an ideal backdrop for your family photos and selfies.

How to perform a puja for Diwali

Growing up, I never paid much attention to the details of how to perform puja at home. That was always the domain of my elders – my *dadi ma* (my dad's mother), my mother, or now my mother-in-law. They graciously and reverently carried out the rituals and recitations, while I observed and did what was asked of me.

Now that I have my own family, I want to honour my family's traditions by learning how to lead puja myself. This will allow me to pass this custom down to my own children, instilling in them the same connection to my beliefs that was gifted to me. Of course, every Hindu family has their own way of conducting puja, which may be built up over generations, and there are no strict rules. I don't presume to instruct others on the 'right' way to practise it; this is simply what I have gleaned from my family. Please consider this a starting guide, for anyone who, like me, wants to keep customs alive for the next generation.

A simple Diwali puja creates a peaceful space to honour traditions. First, tidy up and lay out fresh fruits, sweets, flowers and incense on a clean table. Light *diyas* nearby for a warm glow. Use a thali, silver or brass plate,

light an oil lamp with ghee. Ghee is used in a *diya* to purify the air. It brings joy and promotes peace of mind.

During the ritual, we invite the god Ganesha and goddess Lakshmi in to bless our home and the year ahead.

In Hindu tradition, Lord Ganesha and goddess Lakshmi symbolise two key elements for any new endeavour. Lord Ganesha is revered as the remover of obstacles and patron of fresh starts. He is worshipped to clear any impediments on the path forward. Lakshmi is the goddess of wealth, fortune and beauty. She provides the spiritual and material abundance needed to accomplish goals and find success. Worshipping Ganesha and Lakshmi together blesses a new undertaking with the optimal conditions for growth – a cleared path and prosperous conditions. By honouring these two deities, Hindus draw upon divine wisdom to launch endeavours imbued with the grace and wisdom needed to flourish.

Lakshmi is believed to visit every home during Diwali to bless them with prosperity and wealth. The ritual of a Lakshmi puja is a comprehensive and spiritually enriching ceremony in which Hindus chant mantras and

Hanuman Chalisa (see page 161), ring a puja bell, and sing devotional songs. We offer sincere prayers for prosperity and wisdom in the coming days. We finish the puja with an *aarti* (see page 159), which is an integral part of Indian culture, and offer it to the gods.

During the *aarti*, a lit lamp is circulated in a clockwise rotation before an image of a deity, while participants chant the *aarti*, (the words for the *aarti* are on page 160).

Flower petals are scattered and *prasad* sweets (see below) are given out to close the puja.

After the puja, somebody present will apply *tilak* (see page 12) to the foreheads of all those present using their ring finger. The mark is placed between the two eyebrows. This spot is thought to be a major nerve point in the human body, so placing the mark here is believed to prevent loss of energy.

Finish by tying a *dhaga* (commonly called a *mauli*) – a knotted red thread – around the wrist of all those present. The *dhaga* is typically tied by an elder family member. Good luck and protection are represented by the red thread in Hinduism and the *dhaga* is believed to protect and fight off negative energy. There is also an traditional way to knot this: married ladies have it tied on their left wrist, while males and young girls have it tied on their right. This is done because idols of goddesses are always on the left and idols of gods are always on the right.

Adapt your puja - every household celebrates differently; the focus is on creating a meaningful time for gratitude.

Prasad

Prasad is a sacred offering typically consisting of food that is presented to God as a sign of devotion, then distributed and consumed after praying. Hindus consider *prasad* to be blessed and bestowed with the grace of God. Common temple *prasad* includes sweet rice, fruits, coconut, nuts and special candies. I fondly remember visiting the temples in my childhood and receiving sweet *prasad* like *kheer* (you can find my nanni's recipe on page 59) and *ladoo* (see page 134) as a blessing from the gods.

What to wear on Diwali

According to the Hindu calendar, the festival of Diwali symbolises the new year, and the tradition of wearing new clothes represents new beginnings. As this is such an auspicious occasion, I choose to wear my newest, most vibrant traditional Indian outfits, such as a dress or Indian suit, rather than darker coloured attire. It's a tradition that reflects the embrace of new beginnings and positive energy that this special time of year represents.

What should you gift on Diwali?

This celebration is all about giving and receiving gifts. Traditionally gold items, Indian sweets, nuts and candles are given for prosperity in the coming year. Yet beyond material goods, Diwali gifts represent expressions of affection between loved ones. The act of mindful giving strengthens connections.

For me, gifting homemade sweets, such as *barfi* (see page 136) and *ladoo* (see page 134), during Diwali is deeply personal. The time and care that goes into preparing something yourself adds meaning to the offering and the smile on loved ones' faces when receiving these treats is so satisfying.

How to present and package gifts

This Diwali, express your creativity with gift-wrapping
ideas that use materials you already have
at home to cut down on waste

1. Create distinctive gift wrapping by utilising old newspapers and maps for a vintage-style of wrapping.

2. Use pieces of old saris and tablecloths as inspiration. Simply place the gift item in the centre of the piece of cloth, fold it around the gift and tie a knot. No scissors or tape are needed.

3. Paint boxes, such as old shoe boxes, or delivery boxes that you would normally throw away and decorate them with gems or glitter, then add a ribbon and gift tags (to make your own, see pages 123–127).

4. Arrange smaller goods, such as candies or edible presents, on decorative trays lined with tissue paper.

Diwali gift box
for children

Surprise your little ones on the eve of Diwali with a magical
gift box to spark excitement, and watch their faces light up
as they find thoughtful treats to kindle their celebrations.
This special box overflows with cherished traditions.
I would include some or all of the following:

- a new outfit
- candles and colourful rangoli sand
  (see page 110 for how they can use
  their sand)
- Indian sweets
- decorations, such as hand-painted
  tealights (see page 104)
- a mindful journal for children to jot down
  wishes, prayers and reflections

Countdown checklist

Stay calm and organised in the run-up to Diwali with this helpful four-week countdown checklist. With handy timelines for meal prep, cleaning, decorating and more, this comprehensive guide will help you thoughtfully prepare and cross tasks off your list.

Four weeks before Diwali

☐ Discuss plans with family and friends

☐ Make travel arrangements.

☐ Purchase Diwali cards or start to create them with children (see pages 123–127)

☐ Plan activity time with children to create gifts

Three weeks before

☐ Invite guests

☐ Plan your Diwali menu

☐ Purchase or make Diwali gifts that need to be posted (allowing enough time for delivery)

☐ Organise Diwali outfits

☐ Request time off work (if applicable)

Two weeks before

- [ ] Post cards and gifts
- [ ] Confirm your menu
- [ ] Write a food shopping list
- [ ] Purchase/gather all items for a Diwali box for kids
- [ ] Plan and arrange time to meet family and friends before or during Diwali
- [ ] Create Diwali lanterns and decorations for the house with children

One week before

- [ ] Purchase/gather *diyas*/candles for the house
- [ ] Purchase any gifts for non-family members, e.g. a box of chocolates for a school class
- [ ] Purchase any fireworks

Three days before

- [ ] Clean the house
- [ ] Lay out everyone's clothes
- [ ] Wrap gifts
- [ ] Visit family and friends ahead of Diwali to exchange gifts
- [ ] Make edible gifts mithai and wrap.

Two days before Diwali (*Dhanteras*)

- [ ] Make new purchases for *Dhanteras* (see page 13)
- [ ] Pre-soak your lentils and beans if making *dal makhani* (see page 38)

Countdown checklist

Day before Diwali

- ☐ Start any food preparation, such as chopping
- ☐ Cook any dishes that can then be reheated on the day
- ☐ Make space in the fridge and freezer for any leftovers
- ☐ Create a space for your Diwali puja
- ☐ Purchase fresh flowers.
- ☐ Plan the timing for the day, working out when you need to prepare and cook each element

Diwali

- ☐ Breathe and smile
- ☐ Set the table (ask family members to get involved)
- ☐ Visit your local temple and friends early in the day
- ☐ Pray with an open heart and have the list of *bhajans* at the back of this book available to hand
- ☐ Place candles around the house, ready for you to light later in the evening

Bhajans and aarti

Songs

Aarti is a Hindu worship ritual typically performed daily in homes and temples. It is a key part of puja that seeks blessings. This ritual involves circulating a lit lamp in clockwise rotations before an image of a deity. As the lamp circulates, devotees sing *aarti* hymns in a high, rhythmic tone to create a powerful devotional atmosphere. The songs' lyrics offer effusive praise to the gods. Performing *aarti* imprints these sacred sentiments in the hearts of those gathered through the union of music, light and divinity. This ritual punctuates most Hindu ceremonies and festivals as an act of love and recognition of the divine's constant presence.

Growing up, singing *aarti* and *bhajans* was woven into my daily spiritual practice. My grandma would lead our family in devotional songs and the *aarti* each morning and night, and singing at the temple with the community each week instilled an appreciation for puja that sustains me today. Chanting these hymns

helps quiet the chatter of the mind. While I may now know the words by heart, having the lyrics here serves as a comforting reminder of my roots. Just as this daily practice quietened my mind as a child, singing or reading these devotional songs still helps open my heart to the divine.

I hope including the *aarti* and *Hanuman Chalisa* in this book provides the same gift for you and your family. *Hanuman Chalisa* is one of the most well-known Hindu hymns and honours Lord Hanuman. Chanting this, which consists of 40 verses, is claimed to have many wonderful benefits, including fostering harmony and enhancing wisdom and spiritual knowledge. Additionally, it is meant to remove all the barriers that stand in your path.

Keep the pages bookmarked for all festivities throughout the year and when you need to centre yourself through music and song.

Jai Jagadish
Hare Aarti

Om Jai Jagdish Hare
Swami Jaya Jagdish Hare
Bhakta janon ke sankat (2*)
Kshan me door kar
Om Jai Jagdish Hare

Jo dhyave phal paave
Dhukh vinashe man ka
Swami dhukh vinashe man ka
Sukh sampati Ghar aave (2)
Kashht mite tan ka
Om Jai Jagdish Hare

Mata pita tum mere
Sharan padun mai kis ki
Swami sharan padun mai kis ki
Tum bina aur na dooja (2)
Asha karun mai kis ki
Om Jai Jagdish Hare

Tum puran paramatma
Tum Antaryami
Swami Tum Antaryaami
Para Brahma Parameshwara (2)
Tum sab ke Swami
Om Jai Jagdish Hare

Tum karuna ke saagar
Tum palan karta
Swami Tum palan karta
Mai sevak tum swaami (2)
Kripa karo bharta
Om Jai Jagdish Hare

Tum ho ek agochar
Sab ke pran pati
Swami sab ke prana pati
Kis vidhi milun dayamaya (2)
Tum ko mai kumati
Om Jai Jagdish Hare

Deena bandhu dukh hartaa
Tum rakshak mere
Swami tum rakshak mere
Apne hast uthao (2)
Dwar khada mai tere
Om Jai Jagdish Hare

Vishaya vikar mithao
Paap haro deva
Swami paap haro deva
Shraddha bhakti badhao (2)
Santan ki seva
Om Jai Jagdish Hare

Tan man dhan sab kuch hai tera
Swami sab kuch hai tera
Tera tujh ko arpan (2)
Kya laage mera
Om Jai Jagdish Hare

Om Jai Jagadish Hare
Swami Jai Jagadish Hare
Bhakta janon ke sankat (2)
Kshan me door kare
Om Jai Jagdish Hare

* the number 2 indicates that the line is repeated

Shri Hanuman Chalisa

|| Doha ||

Shri Guru Charan Saroj Raj, Nij manu Mukuru Sudhaari

Barnau Raghubar Bimal Jasu, Jo Daayeku Phal Chaari ||

Buddhiheen Tanu Jaanike,Sumirau Pavan Kumaar |

Bal Buddhi Bidya Dehu Mohi,Harahu Kales Bikaar ||*

|| Chaupai ||

Jai Hanuman Gyaan Gun Sagar |
Jai Kapis Teehun Lok Ujagar ||

Ram Doot Atulit Bal Dhama |
AnjaniPutra Pavansut Nama ||

Mahabir Bikram Bajrangi |
Kumati Nivaar Sumati Ke Sangi ||

Kanchan Baran Biraaj Subesa |
Kaanan Kundal Kunchit Kesa ||

Haath Bajra Aau Dhwaja Biraaje |
Kaandhe Moonj Janeu Saaje ||

Sankar Suvan Kesarinandan |
Tej Prataap Maha Jag Bandan ||

Bidyabaan Guni Ati Chaatur |
Ram Kaaj Karibe Ko Aatur ||

Prabhu Charitra Sunibe Ko Rasiya |
Ram Lakhan Sita Man Basiya ||

Sukshma Roop Dhari Siyahin Dikhawa |
Bikat Roop Dhari Lanka Jarawa ||

Bheem Roop Dhari Asur Sanhaare |
Ramchandra Ke Kaaj Sanwaare ||

Laaye Sajivan Lakhan Jiyaaye |
Shri Raghubeer Harashi Ur Laaye ||

Raghupati Keenhi Bahut Badai |
Tum Mum Priy Bharat Hi Sam Bhai ||

Sahas Badan Tumhro Jas Gaavein |
As Kahi Shripati Kanth Lagavein ||

Sankadik Bramhadi Munisa |
Narad Sarad Sahit Ahisa ||

Jam Kuber Digpaal Jahan Te |
Kabi Kobid Kahi Sake Kahaan Te ||

Tum Upkaar Sugreevhin Kinha |
Ram Milaaye Raajpad Dinha ||

Tumhro Mantra Vibhishan Maana |
Lankeswar Bhaye Sab Jag Jana ||

* the || indicates that the line is repeated

Jug Sahastra Jojan Par Bhaanu |
Lilyo Taahi Madhur Phal Jaanu ||

Prabhu Mudrika Meli
Mukh Maahi |
Jaldhi Laanghi Gaye Achraj
Naahi ||

Durgam Kaaj Jagat Ke Jete |
Sugam Anugraha Tumhre Tete ||

Ram Dooare Tum Rakhwaare |
Hoat Na Aagya Binu Paisare ||

Sab Sukh Lahai Tumhari Sarna |
Tum Rakhshak Kaahu Ko Darna ||

Aapan Tej Samharo Aapai |
Teeno Lok Haank Te Kaanpen ||

Bhoot Pisaach Nikat Nahi Aave |
Mahabir Jab Naam Sunave ||

Naasai Rog Harai Sab Peera |
Japat Nirantar Hanumat Beera ||

Sankat Te Hanuman Chhoodave |
Man Krama Bachan Dhyaan Jo
Laave ||

Sab Par Raam Tapasvi Raja |
Tin Ke Kaaj Sakal Tum Saaja ||

Aur Manorath Jo Koi Laave |
Soi Amit Jivan Phal Paave ||

Chaaro Jug Partaap Tumhara |
Hai Parsiddh Jagat Ujiyara ||

Saadhu Sant Ke Tum Rakhwaare |
Asur Nikandan Ram Dulaare ||

Asht Siddhi Nau Nidhi Ke Daata |
As bar Deen Janki Maata ||

Ram Rasayan Tumhre Paasa |
Sada Raho Raghupati Ke Daasa ||

Tumhre Bhajan Ram Ko Paave |
Janam Janam Ke Dukh Bisraave ||

Antakaal Raghubar Pur Jaayee |
Jahan Janam HariBhakt
Kahayee ||

Aur Devta Chitt Na Dharayi |
Hanumat Sei Sarb Sukh Karayi ||

Sankat Kate Mite Sab Peera |
Jo Sumirai Hanumat Balbira ||

Jai Jai Jai Hanuman Gosaai |
Kripa Karahun Gurudev Ki Naai ||

Jo Sat Baar Paath Kar Koi |
Chhootahin Bandi Maha sukh
Hoyi ||

Jo Yeh Padhe Hanuman Chalisa |
Hoye Siddhi Saakhi Gaurisa ||

Tulsidas Sada Harichera |
Kije Naath Hridaya Mahn Dera ||

|| Doha ||

Pavantanaye Sankat
Haran,Mangal Moorti Roop |

Ram Lakhan Sita Sahit, Hridaya
Basahu Soor Bhoop ||

Mantras

GAYATRI MANTRA

The Gayatri Mantra is one of the most renowned and powerful mantras in Hinduism – a profound hymn of devotion and prayer. The chanting of the Gayatri Mantra is believed to bring success and happiness into one's life, as well as to impart wisdom and enlightenment. The mantra creates a holy basis for various events, from daily devotions to Hindu celebrations, including Diwali.

Om Bhur Bhuvaḥ Suvaha
Tat-savitur Vareñyaṃ
Bhargo Devasya Dheemahi
Dhiyo Yonaḥ Prachodayāt

According to Hindu beliefs, this mantra is usually sung at the closing of your puja ceremony, but it can also be chanted throughout the day, providing many additional benefits, such as purifying the mind and soul, bringing clarity and determination.

Another mantra commonly chanted during religious ceremonies, auspicious events, such as weddings or the start of a new venture, as well as part of daily spiritual practice, is the Sarva Mangala Mangalye, dedicated to Goddess Durga or Parvati, the embodiment of divine strength, devotion and unconditional love.

Sarvamangala mangalye Shive!
Sarvartha Sadhike

Sharanye Tryambake Devi!
Narayani! Namostu Te!

Many seek solace in this mantra when faced with difficulties, believing that its vibrations not only resonate within the physical body but also allow the soul to reach the Goddess's divine energy, capable of alleviating all worldly troubles.

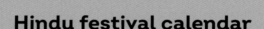

Hindu festival calendar

As our lives get busier, it can be easy to let events
slip by unnoticed, so opposite I have highlighted
some of the important festive dates that you might
want to bookmark – they are the festivals commonly
observed by my family. May this book inspire you to
join in the auspicious observances that resonate most
meaningfully with you throughout the year. Having
the dates handy lets me prepare, clear my schedule
and plan the events that I wish to mark. Due to the
Hindu calendar's adherence to the lunar calendar,
the dates change yearly.

October

Sharad Navratri

Dussehra

Karwa Chauth

Ahoi Ashtami

November

Diwali

Bhai Dooj

January

Lohri

Pongal

February

Mahashivratri

March

Holi

April

Chaitra Navratri
or Vasant

August

India's
Independence Day (15th)

Raksha Bandhan

Krishna Janmashtami
(Lord Krishna's birthday)

September

Ganesh Chaturthi

Hindu festival calendar

Templates

If you don't feel confident drawing
things freehand, or your children need
a little extra help, the next few pages provide
some designs you can trace over to inspire
your crafts. They will be particularly helpful
for the Paper plate Diwali lamps on page 106
and the wrapping paper on page 120.

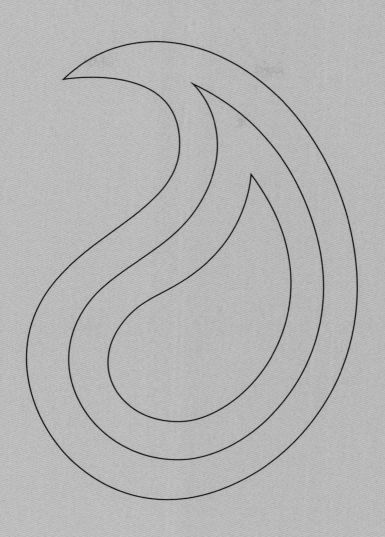

To-do list

- [ ] ....
- [ ] ....
- [ ] ....
- [ ] ....
- [ ] ....
- [ ] ....
- [ ] ....
- [ ] ....
- [ ] ....
- [ ] ....
- [ ] ....
- [ ] ....
- [ ] ....

- [ ]
- [ ]
- [ ]
- [ ]
- [ ]
- [ ]
- [ ]
- [ ]
- [ ]
- [ ]
- [ ]
- [ ]
- [ ]
- [ ]

To-do list

Your traditions and memories

I have left this blank space for you to record your own Diwali memories, traditions, mantras, prayers, and favourite festival foods and recipes. Diwali is a time full of light, family and celebration, but each family has their own unique rituals that make the festival special. Writing them here will allow you to look back on these moments and pass them down to future generations.

173   *Your traditions and memories*

Menu planner

I have left these pages blank for you to design your own Diwali dinner menus. Take inspiration from the recipes shared in this book and create a meal plan that your family and guests will love. You can look back on this in years to come as you establish traditions and add new favourite dishes.

Starters

....

....

....

....

Sides

....

....

....

....

Mains

....

....

....

....

....

....

....

....

....

....

Desserts

....

....

....

....

Drinks

....

....

....

....

NOTES

Other notes

....
....
....
....
....
....
....
....
....
....
....
....
....
....
....

Other notes

Useful stockists and suppliers

STOCKISTS AND SUPPLIERS

Most of the ingredients and equipment you will need in this book are everyday store cupboard staples and common grocery items. However, there may be a few speciality ingredients or tools that require a dedicated shop visit or online purchase.

Below are some of my suggestions for stockists to help you track down anything out of the ordinary.

I've also created a convenient website at celebratediwali.co.uk where you can view all of these recommendations and purchase hard-to-find products directly.

SPICES

I highly recommend Spice Kitchen (spicekitchenuk.com) for all spices, as well as for sourcing beautiful spice *dabba* (spice tins) to store them and keep them fresh.

You can also purchase spices from my website.

CRAFTS

Hobbycraft (hobbycraft.co.uk) and Amazon (amazon.co.uk) are the best places to source all your craft items simply and economically. They have a wide choice of colours, sizes, types of paint etc. and will have everything I've included in the book, from coloured sand to quilling tools for creating your rangoli.

Index

About the author

Renu Bhardwaj's lifelong passion for food and cooking has been a constant source of joy and inspiration. Many of her warmest childhood memories were made gathered around her mother's kitchen in Manchester, the air rich with the aroma of homemade Indian dishes. It was there that Renu's love for the art of food preparation and the power of traditional flavours first took root. Now based in Scotland with her husband Neeraj and their children Arran and Ariya, Renu continues to honour her culinary heritage while also exploring new creative horizons.

Renu has achieved recognition as a leading voice in the food influencer space, being named Scottish Food Influencer of the Year 2024. Her engaging Instagram page has amassed a loyal following, offering viral recipes that blend classic Indian flavours with contemporary Scottish influences. Renu has also leveraged her platform to collaborate with brands aligned with her values of reducing food waste and alleviating the cost of living. She was invited to 10 Downing Street to capture the social media coverage at a special Scottish event.

Acknowledgements

I am truly humbled and filled with gratitude to have had the opportunity to author this book. Bringing a Diwali-themed culinary work to life is a dream I could never have anticipated. Compiling these recipes and crafts has been a profoundly meaningful journey, filled with a mix of emotions – gratitude, pride and a deep appreciation for the cultural heritage that has nourished me.

First and foremost, I want to thank my incredibly supportive husband Neeraj who gave me the encouragement I needed to embark on this book-writing journey. Your unwavering belief in me and willingness to pick up the slack at home, so that I could focus, has been invaluable. This book would not have been possible without your love, patience and support.

To my beautiful children, Arran and Ariya, thank you for checking in and for understanding when Mum needed quiet time to work on her book; your smiles and hugs re-energised me. I hope one day you will read this book and feel proud of what we accomplished as a family. My achievements are our achievements. This book is dedicated to you, my three inspirations. I could not ask for a more loving, patient family. You make every effort worthwhile.

Mum, this book contains more than just recipes and words on a page – it carries the spirit of our family: the treasured dishes passed down from Chai-ji that you would make together in the kitchen, the food that would fill the house, and the joy of gathering around the kitchen table to share a meal. Having you as my mum and first teacher in the kitchen inspired this book. I hope that within these chapters you hear echoes of your guidance and see flashes of the little girl who always wanted to be by your side. To my siblings, I'm so glad I can reflect on our Diwali moments and cherished memories.

I'm extremely thankful to my Glasgow family for shaping

my religious views, guiding and educating me over the last 20 years. It has helped develop my perspective and approach to my culture and religious beliefs over time. Thanks to my closest friends who have been a continual source of encouragement.

To my wonderful online community – you have become true friends. Thank you for your enduring support, uplifting comments and words of encouragement; they have meant the world to me. I am so incredibly grateful for each one of you. I poured my heart into this book, and I hope the recipes feel like shared moments together.

A heartfelt thank you to the incredible team at Ebury who made this book possible. When it wasn't even on my horizon, you believed in me and my story. Celia Palazzo, I'm eternally grateful for your vision, leadership and unwavering support in championing this project from the start. Thank you for bringing together the immensely talented people who worked tirelessly

behind the scenes on editing, design, photography, marketing and more to turn this dream into a reality. To every person involved, your hard work, creativity and dedication brought these pages to life. From the bottom of my heart, thank you all.

Thank you to the generations before me that passed down these traditions. I find so much comfort and meaning in this heritage. My aim is to honour it while giving it new life. To everyone who helped season these recipes and stories with love, my deepest thanks. This book belongs to all of us.

Dear reader, thank you for choosing this book. I hope it becomes your go-to reference and source of inspiration for celebrating Diwali for years to come. May the recipes and memories shared within these pages add meaning and joy to your celebrations. Light and love to you and yours.

1

Pop Press, an imprint of Ebury Publishing
20 Vauxhall Bridge Road
London SW1V 2SA

Pop Press is part of the Penguin Random House group
of companies whose addresses can be found
at global.penguinrandomhouse.com

First published by Pop Press in 2024

www.penguin.co.uk

A CIP catalogue record for this book is available
from the British Library

Hardback ISBN 978 1 529 93415 1

Ebook ISBN 978 1 529 93416 8

Senior Commissioning Editor: Celia Palazzo
Design: Evi-O.Studio | Matt Crawford, Doreen Zheng
and Susan Le
Illustrations: Evi-O. Studio | Matt Crawford, Eloise Myatt,
Siena Zadro and Doreen Zheng
Photography: Luke Albert
Food and Prop Styling: Libby Silbermann
Food and Prop Styling Assistant: Olivia Georgiadis

Printed and bound in Italy by LEGO SpA

Colour origination by Altaimage London

The authorised representative in the EEA
is Penguin Random House Ireland, Morrison Chambers,
32 Nassau Street, Dublin D02 YH68.